T0361557

VETERAN LED

MILITARY LEADERSHIP LESSONS
TO HELP YOUR TEAM
SURVIVE, THRIVE, AND DOMINATE

JOHN S. BERRY

SABREQUILL
PRESS

This book includes recollections of actual events in the author's life. Some conversations have been re-created and/or supplemented. Confidential and privileged information has been protected. The names and details of some individuals have been changed to respect their privacy. This book contains absolutely no legal advice. The strategies and tactics contained herein may not be suitable for your situation. Consult with a professional where appropriate.

Published by Sabrequill Press
Lincoln, Nebraska

Copyright © 2024 John S. Berry

Distributed by Greenleaf Book Group

For ordering information or special discounts for bulk purchases, please contact Greenleaf Book Group at PO Box 91869, Austin, TX 78709, 512.891.6100.

Design and composition by Greenleaf Book Group
Cover design by Trevor Nealy

Publisher's Cataloging-in-Publication data is available.

Print ISBN: 979-8-9905335-0-9

eBook ISBN: 979-8-9905335-1-6

To offset the number of trees consumed in the printing of our books, Greenleaf donates a portion of the proceeds from each printing to the Arbor Day Foundation. Greenleaf Book Group has replaced over 50,000 trees since 2007.

Printed in the United States of America on acid-free paper

24 25 26 27 28 29 30 31   10 9 8 7 6 5 4 3 2 1

First Edition

To all veterans: past, present, and future

CONTENTS

AUTHOR'S NOTE

U pon returning from Vietnam, my father began helping veterans with legal trouble that manifested from their PTSD
symptoms—back then, they called it "shell shock." Veterans often
came to my father for help with a divorce or criminal charges
stemming from untreated PTSD. As a pro bono service, my
father began helping his veteran clients get their VA benefits,
appealing their cases to federal courts when necessary.

A fellow veteran and former client told my father about
"Tommy," a homeless combat veteran who served in Vietnam
and lived under a bridge in a major city with many other homeless veterans. My father felt compelled to help him. Tommy's
drug and alcohol problems stemmed from his untreated PTSD.
Tommy had visited the VA in the 1970s and filed a disability
claim, but the VA failed to adjudicate the claim and never offered
him treatment. By the time my father met him, Tommy had
been homeless for over a decade.

After my father helped him get service-connected for his
PTSD, Tommy began to receive treatment and monthly disability payments from the VA. By the time Tommy received
his correct backpay award, it was hundreds of thousands of

dollars. He bought a house, got sober, got married, and started a business. While Tommy did not find success immediately, he had the skills to be successful the entire decade he lived under the bridge. All veterans possess the same transferrable skills as Tommy. Take charge of your organization and take charge of your future by using the basic leadership skills you learned in the military. You paid the admission fee to enter the world of leadership with your military service. Now it's time to thrive with all you've learned. If you lead like a veteran, you are destined for greatness.

INTRODUCTION

I arrived at 0530, before sunrise, for a quick company meeting followed by physical training. All my platoon's noncommissioned officers (NCOs) had arrived before I stumbled into the company area. They were already planning out the day, coffee in hand, excitedly awaiting first formation. Anxiously, I said, "Morning," knowing they intended to break me or laugh at me. None of them responded; they all just stared at me as if they planned to kill me and eat me for breakfast.

I knew what was coming. First, they would try to smoke me during physical training. After breakfast, they would watch me lead battle drills, critique me, heckle me, and advise me. Over lunch, we would go to the gym and lift weights and then to the motor pool, where I would stand around looking like an idiot all day, trying to be useful without getting in the way. Soon we would go to the field for a thirty-day training exercise, and I trembled at the thought of looking even more incompetent.

I didn't fear spending thirty days and nights in the wilderness with these steely-eyed, barrel-chested killers. I didn't fear my company commander chewing my ass. What I feared was letting these heroes down and being ridiculed by them for the next year. Most of my subordinate leaders had CIBs (Combat Infantryman's Badges) from Desert Storm. As an unproven college kid among men, I felt as useless as wet toilet paper.

In a few months, I would lead this team on my first deployment. What if I screwed up and got someone killed? What if I lost the team's confidence? What if I got us lost and we ended up in a minefield? What if they didn't respect me?

Welcome to leadership, welcome to community, welcome to the military.

My fears came not from my insecurities but from the grave respect and admiration I had for my platoon of proven warriors. These men, the best men I'd ever know, deserved a leader who could keep them safe and make them even better soldiers. As an inexperienced leader, I had no idea how to do this, and that realization terrified me.

If you've ever led a successful team, organization, or company, you remember the terror. You remember the crushing burden, the self-doubt, and the pride of leading a new team. While at the time I dreaded my existence as an inexperienced, incompetent, brand-new infantry platoon leader, I've spent the last twenty-five years of my life trying to get that feeling back. Not the feeling of incompetence but the sense of mission, duty, and community that every veteran remembers. That is where I strive to go every day.

Despite my awareness of my deficiencies, every time I arrived in the Alpha company area with my platoon NCOs, I felt like part of a championship team. Positive attitudes and smiles were everywhere, especially when it sucked. The omniscient, omnipotent NCOs showed up to work in perfectly starched uniforms with glossy, spit-shined combat boots. When we conducted field training, the hypervigilant, detail-oriented professionals started their days with gear secured, weapons clean, vehicles fueled, and equipment inspected. I doubted the relevance of my leadership role on this team of consummate professionals. What I did know: this felt like home, and I was proud to be one of the team.

The feeling of community, dedication, and camaraderie a new platoon leader feels with his first platoon must be experienced to be understood, and I've tried to replicate that feeling in my civilian company. I strive to work in the presence of top-tier professionals who show up every day to give the mission their all and to take care of those in their charge.

After leaving the military, I read over one hundred books on the topics of organizational leadership, professional development, and team building. I hired business coaches, consultants, and industry experts, some of whom I paid up to $25,000 a month. I scoured podcasts, blogs, and YouTube videos, all in search of a mentor to teach me even better leadership lessons than those I learned in the military. No such animal exists.

To be clear, there are no shortages of gurus, experts, consultants, coaches, and authors who can provide a list of leadership principles, tell you how to think, tell you what to do, or repackage and regurgitate something someone else said about leadership. The deficit lies in the number of qualified leaders willing to share the truth about what it takes to lead a great team year over year.

Fortunately, veterans already have the answers. Unfortunately, most don't know it. The answer to sustained great leadership lies in the doing. Leaders earn their roles in the military, and rightfully so. Soldiers train by the numbers, step by painful step, led by a veteran who has personally accomplished exactly what he is instructing his soldiers to do.

This starts day one, in basic training or boot camp, where the highly professional drill sergeant, who proficiently completed each task hundreds of times himself, trains the new private step-by-step in crawl, walk, and run methodology. Once all the recruits demonstrate proficiency in the task, the team moves to the next task. While some military tasks take years to master, the entire organization attains a base level of competence and relentlessly trains on those basic blocking and tackling skills for their entire careers. Shoot, move, and communicate.

This methodology differs from anything you can learn on YouTube or in a consultant-led "discovery day" or a business "boot camp." Military leaders do not lead with theories or thoughts; they lead with actions and results. They improve through hypercritical, brutally honest feedback. In the military, you can't "pay to play." Every opportunity, every promotion, and every victory must be earned. As one excited battle buddy exclaimed, "You can't pay for this experience unless you have a DoD-sized budget. Imagine the cost of firing the weapon systems, building the teams, and daily training."

The military invests in its leaders, preparing them for bigger opportunities with meticulously designed career paths. In most cases, service members who do not move up in the ranks get moved out of the ranks. But it starts the same for every military leader.

All of us who joined the United States military began our development upon hearing the command "Drop!" And if you were like me, you heard it thousands of times. For those of you who haven't served, "Drop!" means stop what you are doing immediately, get in the "front-leaning rest position," and prepare to start doing push-ups. "Did I tell you to start pushing?"

"Drop!" is a corrective action with a physical manifestation. Pain is a teaching tool. And while civilians may think "dropping" someone is a degrading command because it could be an embarrassing public shaming, when you get "dropped," you don't care too much about the embarrassment; you're too busy doing push-ups and trying to figure out what you did wrong.

Somewhere in the midst of muscle fatigue and fear, lessons crystallize in our minds. And until those lessons control our actions, we feel them in various forms of pain and exhaustion. When we would reach muscle failure from doing push-ups, if the sergeant knew we had not yet learned the lesson, we would receive the instruction to roll over onto our backs and do flutter kicks. When we could no longer keep our legs six inches off the ground, we were allowed to stand up and "beat your boots." Squat down, slap your boots with your hands, stand up, and repeat—one hundred times.

If you've ever been "dropped," you already know that the sergeant, the noncommissioned officer (NCO), is the backbone of the United States military. As the saying goes, officers plan, sergeants execute. Sergeants are responsible for training America's sons and daughters to the highest standards of competence to reduce the number of injuries in training and deaths in combat.

Throughout my military career, I was inspired, mystified, and fearful of the leadership of sergeants. To many of us, sergeants are superheroes with abilities to read minds, know the future, see through wall lockers, and perform logistical miracles. In hindsight, the real superpower wielded by sergeants was to train, lead, and transform others. In Hollywood, we see the battle-hardened sergeant transform the pudgy, lazy, cowardly recruit into a rippling, dead-eyed killer after just eight weeks of boot camp. While the Hollywood transformation is not entirely accurate, it's not patently false. Sergeants are gods of leadership and human transformation.

I spent my military career trying to gain the trust of sergeants. When I was a cadet or student, I wanted them to trust my potential. As a commissioned officer, I wanted them to trust my leadership. I knew that if my sergeants respected me, I would succeed, and I also knew that if the sergeants did not support me, I would fail. The great lesson of military leadership is that you can be the most competent leader in the world, but the success of the mission will be determined by those in your charge, not you. If your team sucks, you will fail. If you suck but have strong subordinate leaders, chances are good that you will succeed in spite of yourself or your poor decisions. As an army officer, I saw mediocre leaders achieve amazing results because they trusted their sergeants.

If I have not already made it clear, I have believed, since the beginning of my military career, that the approval of the sergeant under my charge was tantamount to success. I admired my sergeants and constantly feared failing them.

When I learned I was going to be leading a platoon run by Desert Storm combat veterans, I knew I was not going to show up without some form of credibility. I was a newly minted second lieutenant. A kid with a college degree sent to lead combat veterans in their field of expertise. It's not that I felt inadequate to lead these heroes because I lacked confidence. Objectively, I lacked the experience and knowledge to do anything other than be their student, their shadow, their intern. I did not deserve to be on their team, and now I was their named leader. Positional leadership—a fictional construct—gives you a title, but everyone knows who is really in charge. And in the army, sergeants are always in charge.

I am about to tell you what sergeants know.

The lessons I learned from the backbone of the army helped me build an eight-figure business that has reached the *Inc.* 5000 list of the fastest-growing companies in the United States seven years in a row. We achieved this by developing a culture of winning and leadership. Today, we actively recruit former sergeants and officers. Veterans make up over 30 percent of our team. We have won the Department of Labor HIRE Vets Platinum Medallion Award and the Employer Support of the Guard and Reserve Pro Patria Award. We have been recognized as a *Military Times* Best for Vets employer and a VETS Indexes Recognized Employer. Our formula is simple: lead with simple military principles, and hire veterans who understand those principles to lead the organization.

My father, also a veteran and the founder of our company, preached repeatedly, "You can't get rich off your own time." He was not just talking about money. The lessons you learned from sergeants will certainly help you create wealth through leading high-functioning, successful teams. But richness in life comes from following and leading others in challenging times. There is no greater wealth than being a member of an unstoppable team.

Need results? Team not executing? Anybody can plan; anybody can dream. Few can execute with the violent proficiency of the United States military. If you served, nothing in this book will shock you. This book is not just for the dog-faced infantry soldier but for anyone who served in any branch, whether you were the tip of the spear or in the rear with the gear. For readers who didn't serve, and those who "almost" served, the book may provide you with leadership lessons and insights that demonstrate why hiring veterans is crucial to the success of your organization.

I served as an active-duty infantry officer, but I also served as a logistics officer and as a member of the reserve component during a twenty-year military career. I was deployed twice and had two company commands and a battalion command. Despite all this experience, most of the lessons in this book, the most valuable ones that I use today to run my company, I learned during my first three years in the military as a lieutenant.

I struggled for several years as a civilian running a business. Sometimes it was as simple as not having enough cash in the bank to make payroll. Other times, we lost or terminated key employees and scrambled to keep the business running, restructuring the entire team to ensure we met our obligations to our clients.

During the years that we struggled to survive, my military leadership lessons haunted me. Every new problem seemed to be solvable with a lesson from the military. Yet I ignored my instincts and my training.

During a drill weekend in the National Guard, I spoke with my commander, who was a scrum master for a large company, about not only my challenges of running the day-to-day business but also my failed attempts to build for the future. My commander explained how he employed basic military lessons at a company much larger than mine. I thought that if it worked for him, it could work for me. It did.

This book is divided into three parts: "Survive," "Thrive," and "Dominate." In the military, we first learn to survive through basic individual skills training. Once we master individual survival skills, we qualify for the opportunity to lead a team. If you cannot survive on your own, you cannot lead a team. In the "thrive" phase, we work through military lessons on team building and team-level execution. Formidable organizations are composed of great teams. This is where we create the opportunity to dominate our adversaries or objectives with high-functioning, mission-oriented teams just like we did as teams in the military.

At the end of each chapter, you will find the "After-Action Review" (AAR) section. You may recall conducting an AAR after every mission or training exercise. During the AAR, we restated the mission and talked about what was supposed to happen, what actually happened, what actions we should sustain, and opportunities for improvement. At the end of each chapter, I use the abbreviated AAR methodology, summarizing three "sustains" and three "improves" that I found valuable. The "sustains" are lessons I learned and implemented quickly and successfully. The "improves" are areas where I still struggle or have fallen short repeatedly. I acknowledge that I do not have all the answers and that what worked for me may not work for others. The real value is not in the lesson but in the habit of capturing lessons learned and reexamining them from time to time.

Part I

SURVIVE

1

SITUATIONAL AWARENESS

A leader is a man who can adapt
principles to circumstances.

—Attributed to George S. Patton

On patrol you keep your head on a swivel, constantly looking for threats. You know that long before you encounter the enemy, you will likely see several signs of enemy presence. You also know that if you get complacent and stop looking, the enemy will surprise and kill you. Before you started the patrol, you briefed your team with the intelligence (intel) report, which told you exactly what the enemy was doing several hours or days ago. But you know that intel is not always accurate, and stale intel is rarely reliable. You must be mentally present and alert at all times, regardless of what you know about the past.

This situational awareness training started the day you got off the bus at boot camp or basic training. After the initial drill sergeant shark attack, just when you thought it was safe, a drill sergeant popped up out of thin air to politely inform you that you had made another mistake. Perhaps you walked in the grass, talked during chow, or failed to square a corner. The next thing you knew, you were in the front-leaning rest waiting to push your chest to the sidewalk until muscle failure.

After a few days you learned that if you did something wrong, a drill sergeant would catch you doing it. After a few weeks you learned that if you developed situational awareness of drill sergeants' locations, you would know how to avoid them and all the pain that came with a close encounter. This doesn't necessarily mean you were trying to sham or beat the system (but you probably were); it means you began to understand your environment well enough to know when you were most vulnerable.

When I went through Army Ranger School, the Ranger Instructors (RIs) were like super drill sergeants. The RIs seemed to know everything that happened on a patrol. They critiqued every movement; and if one of your team members failed, they let you know that you as the leader failed to observe and correct the shortcoming. If you were lucky, the RIs would just smoke you with endless push-ups and flutter kicks. If you were unlucky, you either failed out of the course or received a "major minus" mark in your file, which also made it more likely that you would fail out, but not till the end of the three-week phase you were currently suffering through.

The RIs relentlessly swarmed like killer bees during the first week of Ranger School, encouraging weak candidates to quit and dropping others from the course for failing to achieve passing scores on a variety of highly scrutinized physical fitness tests. After the first week, the RIs' focus shifted to meticulously evaluating our abilities to successfully lead a patrol to Ranger standards. With all the weak candidates gone, the RIs targeted the incompetent. Ranger School simulates combat stress by depriving you of food and sleep. You learn quickly that if anyone becomes hungry or tired enough, they become incompetent.

After we survived the three-week Fort Benning Phase, we advanced to the Blue Ridge mountains near Dahlonega, Georgia. During the first week of Mountain Phase, we stayed in an open barracks and spent our days learning mountaineering skills such as rappelling, tying every type of knot, and climbing the face of a cliff known as Mount Yonah.

By this point in our training, most of us had lost a significant amount of body weight and felt starved every day. Some students would sneak over to the dumpsters at night and dive in, hoping to find a half-eaten chicken leg that the well-fed on-site medics had discarded. While the school prohibited this type of conduct, it happened, and those who had situational awareness got away with it.

However, dumpster diving was nothing compared to a story I heard from a fellow lieutenant, which was confirmed with harsh warnings from the Mountain Phase Ranger Instructors. One night, a group of daring Ranger students (all second lieutenants) executed a brilliant plan to sneak out of the training area and take a taxi to the Walmart in town to buy multiple duffel bags' worth of contraband food that they would hide in the barracks and share with their fellow Ranger students.

Surprisingly, the young lieutenants executed a flawless escape and evasion, changed into civilian clothes, including hats to cover their shaved heads, and spent hundreds of dollars on beef jerky, nuts, candy, and other calorie-dense foods. The lieutenants snuck back into Camp Merrill and shared their bounty with the other Ranger students in the barracks. Using flawless situational awareness, they knew the precise time when the RIs would be in a change-of-shift meeting and where they could exit the camp without being seen.

Had the tale of the Walmart Rangers ended here, it would have been one of audacity and cunning situational awareness. Unfortunately, upon sharing in the lieutenants' spoils, a couple of "bat boys" (junior enlisted Ranger battalion soldiers) believed they too could escape, trek to Walmart, and return undetected with even more boodle. The next night, they executed a similar plan, but instead of changing into civilian clothes, they put civilian clothes over portions of their uniforms and failed to cover their bald heads. Upon their exit from Walmart, a security guard, who had previously worked at Camp Merrill, noticed the bat boys' bald heads, emaciated bodies, and partial uniforms, and called the Ranger Training Battalion to let them know a few students had just left the store.

As you can imagine, the Walmart Rangers got caught and were kicked out of Ranger School. Aside from the obvious issues of lack of integrity, cheating, and breaking the rules, a lesson about situational awareness can be gleaned. Not only had the lieutenants planned to sneak out during hours of limited visibility when the RIs were in a meeting, but they also understood that if anyone in town saw their bald heads or any portion of their uniforms, their mission could be compromised. In this case, the situational awareness meant the difference between an undetected trip to Walmart, with a triumphant return to share calorie-rich food with starving Ranger students, and getting caught and getting several fellow Rangers kicked out of the school.

Situational awareness is not about avoiding getting caught doing something wrong. During my time as a criminal defense attorney, I learned that professional criminals know that it is only a matter of time before they get caught, regardless of the amount of situational awareness they exercise. Situational awareness is about understanding ever-present threats, continual risk, and information about your opportunities and constraints.

SITUATIONAL AWARENESS IN BUSINESS

On patrol we constantly sent information to leaders to keep them aware of our situation so they could maintain visibility of the battlefield. We called in SITREPs (situational reports) periodically or upon request. Internally, after we completed actions on any objective, we would gather ACE reports to learn the status of our team's ammo, casualties, and equipment. Every day for resupply we submitted a LOGSTAT report so the logisticians responsible for our sustainment had situational awareness of what we had on hand and what we would need for the next seventy-two hours, including food, fuel, ammunition, and medical supplies.

Just as in the military, in business, situational awareness is key to survival. At Berry Law we used to do a SWOT (strengths, weaknesses, opportunities, and threats) analysis every year but then would totally forget about it after two months and lose awareness of both opportunities and threats throughout the year. We became much more effective and profitable when we reviewed the SWOT analysis at weekly meetings and maintained our situational awareness.

Even as a small organization, we paid a heavy price for lack of situational awareness. First, we didn't know or understand our financial numbers. We generally knew the amount of money we had to bring in each month to meet overhead expenses, but we didn't understand the basics. We didn't know what metrics team members had to meet for the company to generate a profit or for the individual employees to generate a bonus. We simply held our breath until the end of the year and then paid any money left over to the team as a bonus and celebrated. If we lost money at the end of the year, we just called it a bad year and blamed the economy, a business cycle, or some other uncontrollable force. Some years, our situational awareness was so poor we even paid bonuses when we lost money because we didn't understand that money in the bank did not equate to profit. We flew so blind that we borrowed money to pay bonuses and didn't know it.

Over the years, we learned how leading indicators could increase our situational awareness. Today's numbers could be used to forecast tomorrow's cash. We became aware of the number of leads we needed to fill our sales pipeline, the amount of time it took to service clients, and what had to happen at every phase of a case for us to properly do our jobs. We learned how to determine cost per lead, cost per acquisition of a client, lifetime value of a client, the cost to properly service a client, and the cost of client turnover. Most importantly, we learned that the most expensive mistake was hiring cheap employees. Situational awareness grows from both learning and experience. Unfortunately, you cannot just go to college, read a few books, and—boom—develop situational awareness.

As taught in the military, the survival skill of situational awareness must be learned and honed through specific experiences. We learn about it on the first day of boot camp or basic training. We learn to be aware of lurking drill sergeants who painfully teach us how to pay attention to detail. In combat training, we learn from proven military leaders what to look for on a patrol.

In business, our basic survival skills lead us to inspect operations and gather and analyze data, which we synthesize into reports. We constantly monitor our clients' needs and future needs as well as our competitors' moves. But, as I have learned, that is not enough; and it's one of the reasons leaders must be present in an organization to have true situational awareness.

Early on in our business, I served the company best as a technician rather than as a manager or leader. We trusted a longtime bookkeeper who came in early and stayed late. She rarely took more than a couple of days' vacation at a time. Back in those days, I worried mostly about the amount of money coming into the business and paid less attention to the amount of money going out. I blindly assumed that our accountant would catch any irregularities and bring them to our attention.

As our company grew, it seemed that our accountant's office never responded in a timely manner. The bookkeeper warned us the accountant might shutter his business soon. Not wanting to take any chances, we terminated the accountant and hired a larger accounting firm. The new accountant asked me many questions I could not answer, so I suggested he speak directly with the bookkeeper. A couple months later, the accountant told me that I needed to come to his office.

When I arrived, the accountant first said that he had audited our trust account and that everything was in perfect order. I expected this, because as an attorney I paid close attention to the trust account to ensure that I complied with all attorney ethics rules. Then came the bad news. The accountant showed me records from our general account, which had tens of thousands of dollars of unexplained expenses.

I was livid. I could not believe our loyal bookkeeper would steal from the firm. Then I felt a hollow feeling of disappointment in myself for not having had the situational awareness to know that this had been going on for several years. As we dug deeper, it turned out that the bookkeeper had not stolen any money; she simply wasn't a competent bookkeeper. She didn't know the difference between costs and expenses and lacked the ability to organize the firm's finances.

Of course, over the years, I can recount several of my failures to maintain situational awareness within the company. Fortunately, even though that caused us to bleed cash from time to time, we survived.

On a much larger scale, lack of situational awareness killed industry leaders Kodak and Blockbuster. Kodak was once a household name that revolutionized the photography and videography industries, but its leaders refused to respond to the growing popularity of digital photography, even though Kodak engineers first developed the technology. Kodak's leaders continued to promote their analog products and decided against making the transition to digital when they were poised to continue dominating both markets. Their lack of situational awareness let dominance slip from their grasp.

Blockbuster, the nation's dominant video rental chain, seemed unstoppable in the 1990s. But its lack of situational awareness regarding the rapid technological advances guiding consumer behavior led to bankruptcy in 2010. The CEO's insistence that Redbox and Netflix couldn't come close to their brick-and-mortar profits made for a lagging response to the rapidly shifting consumer trend. They not only missed an opportunity to expand their place in the market but were also forced to close their doors.

Conversely, following are some examples of veteran-led companies that had the situational awareness to not only survive but ultimately dominate.

Federal Express, founded by veteran Frederick W. Smith, a marine who earned the Silver Star and two Purple Hearts during two tours in Vietnam, demonstrated keen situational awareness in the early years of the internet. Understanding the changing operating environment, Federal Express rebranded itself as FedEx and launched fedex.com as the first transportation and logistics website. It was the first site to offer online package tracking, which allowed customers to conduct business over the internet. The situational awareness of the impact the internet would have on the world led to FedEx becoming an early adopter and industry leader.

Army Reserve officer and Nike founder Phil Knight recognized that he needed to shift his company's focus from design and manufacturing to marketing and branding when the Nike brand began to decline in the mid-1980s. Up until that time, Knight and his cofounder, World War II veteran Bill Bowerman, previously focused on design and quality to get the shoes on star athletes and manufacturing to keep the shoes affordable for consumers. They adjusted this strategy to keep consumers coming back. Nike's slogans became part of our culture, and the Air Jordan brand expanded Nike's domain. Knight's situational awareness at a time when the company had already reached $1 billion in revenue was essential in keeping the brand relevant and growing for decades to come.

SITUATIONAL AWARENESS AND ENVIRONMENT

During Operation Iraqi Freedom and Operation Enduring Freedom, "current operating environment" became a ubiquitous buzz phrase in high-level briefings. If all military units in the area of operations were to have a common operating picture (COP), they needed to understand the ever-changing environment in which they operated.

When we deploy, we learn about the culture of our host nation, their rich histories and traditions, their economy, currency,

Learning about the current operating environment

languages, and their allegiances. When I deployed to Iraq, we learned about the Shia and Sunni conflict as well as the conflict between the Arabs and the Persians. During my deployment to Bosnia, we learned about how the fall of a united Yugoslavia led to a war among the Muslim Bosnians, the Serbs, and the Croatians. Situational awareness of current operating environment can be much more actionable if you also understand its history.

What's going on in your market today? What does the history of the market tell you about potential trends? Who are the entrenched competitors? Who are your potential allies who could increase your effectiveness through partnerships and collaborations?

One key to situational awareness in military operations includes understanding the "enemy situation," which I always felt was the highlight of the first paragraph of the army operations order. Before we put our soldiers in harm's way, we wanted to know the strength and disposition of the enemy. Sometimes the enemy aggressively set ambushes, used snipers, or planted IEDs (improvised explosive devices). Other times, the enemy displayed minimal hostile activities, and we planned accordingly. When the enemy changed their tactics and began remote-detonating IEDs or using VBIEDs (vehicle-borne IEDs), we needed situational awareness to respond in a manner that mitigated risk and protected fellow service members.

In business, the enemy situation is not always about what your competitors are doing to win the market and ensure your demise. Sometimes the actions of your competitors do not even pose a threat. On multiple occasions I observed new competitors come into our markets with massive advertising campaigns. While my initial reaction was fear that our competitors would put us out of business, the numbers told a different story. Contrary to our expectations, when competitors spent large amounts of money on marketing, we saw an increase in demand for our services. Essentially, our competitors created more awareness of our services in the marketplace and educated the consumers for us.

When my former chief operating officer served as cavalry platoon leader in Iraq, his battalion commander told him that while on patrol, he should constantly be thinking about the worst thing that could possibly happen to the platoon and how he would react if it did. Acting quickly in adverse situations can save you from more dire outcomes. Contemplate pitfalls and plan for them. Conduct tabletop drills for things like IT outages, liability-driven events, cash shortfalls, and any other problem that, if not solved swiftly and effectively, could stop your company dead in its tracks.

Sometimes the greatest threat comes not from the enemy, but from new government regulations that drive up your operating costs. Maybe your friendly economy takes a downturn, providing both obstacles and opportunities. In other words, the danger you face may not come from an adversary but from a changing condition in your industry or in the economy. You must have the situational awareness to respond as necessary.

As retail giant Amazon became the go-to location for online shopping, many small businesses folded. These businesses saw Amazon as the enemy. Aldevra, a veteran-owned small business founded by service-disabled marine Rodney Marshall, didn't see a threat but an opportunity. Using Amazon's capabilities to highlight the company's diversity certifications in medical and foodservice equipment, Aldevra was able to effectively market its products to enterprise businesses with specific sourcing needs and requirements, earning it a spot on *Inc.*'s Vet 100 list.

Equally important as understanding the enemy situation is understanding the "friendly situation." What's going on in your community? Where can you help? Where can you provide value? Where can you build a community of consumers for your product or service? Does that community already exist? Understanding where your objectives may be aligned with another noncompetitor in your battle space may provide for an opportunity to share resources, collaborate, and even build a community.

My ignorance about how to collaborate with allies cost me

several opportunities over the years—opportunities on which my competitors capitalized. I missed a huge trade show opportunity. I turned down a speaking engagement, which would have put me in front of hundreds of potential customers. Instead of understanding how other industries may have the same consumers that we serviced, I only sought opportunities in my industry. My lack of situational awareness came at a steep price in lost opportunities.

SITUATIONAL AWARENESS AND OPPORTUNITY

I never wanted to become support platoon leader. Like all infantry lieutenants, I expected to go from being a line platoon leader to the scout platoon leader. Even worse, shortly after I learned I would be leaving my line platoon to become support platoon leader, our brigade had a rotation at the National Training Center (NTC) in ninety days. The battalion had not yet qualified on most of its weapon systems, and a continental United States–wide ammo shortage meant we would not get all the ammo we forecasted.

At the time, the S3 (operations officer) seemed hell-bent on getting all our MK-19 (automatic grenade launcher) gunners qualified so they could shoot at NTC. The problem was that, contrary to his forecasts and requests, Fort Hood had no MK-19 ammo on base. When I told the S3 about the ammo shortage, he looked at me with sleep-deprived raccoon eyes and said, "I know that. Go buy a case of Jack Daniels and make a drug deal with other support platoon leaders in this division. Sweeten the deal with a bottle of Jack."

In the military garrison environment, a "drug deal" happened when two units swapped assets to make a training event happen. For example, transportation units regularly lent mechanized infantry units the trucks they needed for gunnery in exchange for the 5.56 ammo that infantry units received in gluttonous quantities. The drug deal ensured the infantry units got trucks for task force missions, and it ensured the transportation units would have enough ammo to qualify their soldiers on the firing range.

After reaching out to every MTOE (modified table of organization and equipment) unit at Fort Hood, I befriended an armor officer who, like me, had performed too well as line platoon leader and been stuck with the support platoon leader job. We had initially met in Croatia on R&R during our Bosnia deployment during a drinking competition with some British officers on the beaches of Makarska. We reminisced about the Bosnia deployment and then commiserated about the lack of MK-19 ammo. Two weeks later, the armor officer called me. He excitedly said something about the Texas National Guard, the Waco reenactment, and a bunch of other stuff that made no sense until he said, "I got Mark 19 ammo, and I may have some extra for ya, but here's what I need from you . . ."

His situational awareness of events outside of active-duty Fort Hood (now Fort Cavazos) somehow got him the ammo. I had confined my search to active-duty armor and infantry units, yet he knew to look for opportunity elsewhere.

Your situational awareness protects you from threats and

shows you opportunities. However, if you plan to capitalize on your awareness, you must do so before the opportunity passes you by. You must move with a sense of urgency. Situational awareness does not tell you how long the opportunity will last.

SITUATIONAL AWARENESS AND PEOPLE

One of the most difficult aspects of situational awareness to master is understanding people and their motives. I think back to training for deployments, and learning which organizations and people may have been sympathetic to our cause and which were likely to be hostile. It wasn't only about fighting one enemy to the death; it was about understanding the dynamic political and economic factors that influenced the key players. We learned that one group of people might be friendly to the U.S. military today, but they could turn on us tomorrow for a myriad of reasons which we did not control.

One of the biggest threats to your organization will always be people who take actions to harm you, when you have taken no action to invoke their wrath. Some vendors will take advantage of the information they learn from you and use it against you to get hired by your competitor. Some well-meaning allies will get into deep trouble and unintentionally drag you down with them. People will scheme to rip you off on day one, while others make that decision years into the relationship because of jealousy or financial hardship. You may even face a coup from within your own team to remove you from your leadership position or steal your clients.

SITUATIONAL AWARENESS SOLUTIONS

So how do you maintain situational awareness when so much could go wrong? I've found that if you can maintain situational awareness in four areas, you will know when to expect incoming rounds and prepare for their impact. These four areas are (1) data and performance metrics, (2) financial reports, (3) culture, and (4) leadership team.

Data and Performance Metrics

Know your metrics both inside and outside the organization. Look at external numbers and data from your industry and markets. While any anomalies in your numbers could come from external forces, you must also check internal performance metrics to determine the cause of the irregularity. It's easy to blame competitors and market conditions, but understanding whether your team is hitting performance metrics will help you determine whether the enemy is inside the gate or out. More on this to come in future chapters.

Financial Reports

Understand basic financial reports. If you don't know how to read a balance sheet, profit and loss statement, or a budget variance report, learn. The numbers always tell a story. If you can't read the numbers, you won't know the story, and you will lack the situational awareness to protect the financial health of your company.

Culture

When you intentionally develop your team culture, you set behavior standards, rhythm, levels of professionalism, and productivity expectations. Culture is your organizational identity. Situational awareness of your culture will lead you to opportunities for growth and improvement that you won't always see in your data or financial reports.

Leadership Team

A strong, aligned leadership team of competent captains will provide you frequent communication about everything you need to know inside and outside of your organization. However, if your leadership team fractures and develops silos, politics, and a rumor mill, your situational awareness will suffocate in a toxic cloud of distrust and gamesmanship. Before long, you won't know who is competent and who is not, who is truthful and who is deceitful.

Finally, we all have blind spots. We never see the entire picture by ourselves. Our situational awareness can be affected by our biases, expectations, past experiences, fears, and optimism. Taking a buddy team approach helps us better understand our current operating environment.

Think of a platoon on patrol. Sometimes the front of the platoon finds the threat. Other times one of the flanks is the first to observe the enemy prior to contact. Even those in the rear of the formation may become aware of a danger or opportunity that the rest of the platoon missed. Opportunity, like warfare, has become asymmetrical.

Without a team, you must accept that your situational awareness is limited to, at most, two eyes, two ears, one nose, and one brain. Your chances of survival increase when you have a buddy, or several, to help you see, hear, and smell more than just what you are searching for. Opportunities do not come in a linear and proportionate manner. The more eyes looking for them, the better. Just as lack of situational awareness allows the enemy to flank you, it also allows opportunity to bound past you. The more situationally aware the team, the more eyes and ears look for threats and opportunities. Your personal situational awareness is never enough to see all the enemy threats and all the opportunities simultaneously.

AFTER-ACTION REVIEW

Sustain

1. Situational awareness means understanding your data. Know your numbers.

2. Awareness of your operating environment provides awareness of opportunities and dangers.

3. Know what's going on in your community and observe opportunities to provide value.

Improve

1. Situational awareness does not mean knowing or under-standing everything all the time. Learn what's most important and pay attention.

2. Know the locations of the drill sergeants. If you don't know key players, laws, and regulations, you may be unknowingly setting yourself up to fail.

3. Leverage the observations of a buddy, or better yet a team, to see what you cannot.

2

BUDDY SYSTEM

Coming together is a beginning. Keeping together is progress.
Working together is success.

—Attributed to Henry Ford

On day one, the drill sergeant assigns you a buddy. You never leave your buddy. You eat with your buddy, you train with your buddy, you go to the showers with your buddy, you go to the latrine with your buddy. Bottom line: you never go anywhere alone, and you never leave your buddy.

While it is true that the United States military never leaves a fallen comrade on the battlefield, "no soldier left behind" starts with the buddy system. The buddy system teaches safety, accountability, and strength in numbers. I feel a lot safer out in the middle of nowhere if I have a buddy with me: two rifles have more firepower than one, and, in most cases, two people have more brainpower than one. (But if you've served in the military, you've met the buddy team that shares one brain.)

In life, in the military, and in business, you need a buddy to survive.

The buddy system serves as the entry barrier to leadership: if you can't work with your single assigned buddy, you will never lead a team. The first building block for leadership development is to lead one person. I hear wanna-preneuers talk about leading large companies, yet they can barely lead themselves. If you can't lead yourself, you cannot lead another person, and if you can't lead one person, you will never lead one hundred. This is why all leadership starts with the buddy system.

If your buddy is stronger and smarter, you will get stronger and smarter because you do everything together. If your buddy is dumber and weaker, hopefully you can make him stronger and smarter. Many studies have found that high-performing groups succeed at levels far beyond any individual's ability, proving that group synergy is real, measurable, and effective.

And yes, you will be assigned buddies who come to you as dead weight. You must improve that buddy or you will carry that dead weight with you. If you let your buddy drag you down, you will feel that pull toward hell every day. There is nothing worse than starting the day with an oxygen thief for a buddy.

Think back to basic or boot camp: The unfortunate soldier stuck with the dead-weight buddy got smoked right alongside their buddy. Every time the weaker buddy screwed up, which happened all day every day, the other buddy paid. Babysitting that buddy through physical training, chow, training, latrine duty, kitchen patrol duty, barracks cleaning, weapons cleaning, and formation is enough to make anyone want to quit.

Sometimes it's even worse with the buddy who refuses to comply with the buddy system. I understand that some people work better alone. Many highly proficient technicians lack people skills. They go through life gifted with exceptional hard technical skills and cursed with weak people skills—not everyone is suited for leadership. The loner who doesn't like the buddy system can be a productive team member, but she will never lead the organization.

The military, like business, is built for efficiency. To operate efficiently as humans, we must be able to work together to benefit from each other's talents to achieve a larger goal. Getting from point A to point B as rapidly and efficiently as possible requires teamwork, and usually a lot of shared discomfort.

For example, military transportation to training areas is the game of packing as many bodies into small spaces as humanly possible. Cattle trailers drive us around base. To fill a trailer, sergeants yell out, "Make your buddy smile." By this your sergeant means to get close—to squeeze together closer than you ever imagined possible, with rucksacks on, because no matter how full the trailer gets, we keep filling it until everybody is in.

Getting close means getting so close that you're basically standing in the boots of your fellow soldier. Even standing in line at the chow hall: "Move closer—close the gaps." We're expected to feel the breath of others against our neck as we stare at the back of the shaved head in front of us.

If you served in the infantry, you know all about spooning at the listening post/outpost (LPOP) under a shared poncho liner. The common goal of not freezing to death seems to break down any barriers you may have been experiencing. As your shaking body clings to your buddy for warmth, your shared misery creates a stronger bond. Cold, wet misery loves the company of another cold, wet body, which miraculously, when combined, generates enough heat to survive.

There's something to be said about being so uncomfortably close to someone that every movement you make could affect their comfort or discomfort. The bonds we form in the military are unlike any others we experience throughout our lives, but we can transpose some of those same lessons onto our business and personal relationships outside of service.

I still have strong bonds with colleagues with whom I worked on tough projects or long jury trials; or had moments of prolonged mutual suffering where we spent almost every minute of every day together to accomplish a mission. Unfortunately, as a civilian in temperature-controlled rooms, I have never felt the closeness of crawling under a poncho liner with a colleague and shivering through the night together.

NOT ALL BUDDIES ARE ASSIGNED

I entered Ranger School right after graduating from Airborne School in December 1998. I recognized a guy in my platoon from Infantry Officers Basic Course named Jeremy. Jeremy, a West Point graduate, sought to become a third-generation Ranger. His grandfather, a World War II Ranger, stormed the beaches of Normandy, and his father, also Ranger qualified, fought in Vietnam.

In Ranger School, the instructors starve you and deprive you of sleep as you go through the training to simulate combat stress. Back then, the rules allowed Ranger students a limited amount of tobacco products per phase. Most of the students used Copenhagen or other forms of chewing tobacco to stay awake. Because you can't smoke while patrolling, most smokers became chewers. I didn't like "dip" because it made me feel dehydrated. However, on the advice of several Ranger School alumni, I showed up with the maximum amount of tobacco products allowed for each phase.

Without the comforts of food and sleep, tobacco users became tobacco fiends. I carried my authorized tobacco ration to help my buddies who usually ran out of their allotment near the end of the phase when they needed it most. I didn't want to fail a patrol because a member of my squad or platoon could not stay awake.

Toward the end of Benning Phase at Camp Darby, Jeremy ran out of tobacco. At the time, I had been assigned platoon leader for the next patrol, and I assigned Jeremy to create my sand table, a terrain model to visualize a tract of territory. You can't conduct a good operations order without a great sand table, and Jeremy created the best. When briefing starving, half-asleep Rangers, you can't just tell them what to do, you must show them, and I planned to do so on one of Jeremy's meticulous sand tables.

Jeremy created the perfect sand table for me. I observed clearly decipherable terrain features that mirrored our topographical map, perfect placement of icons, exact directional orientation of the table, and yarn in perfect squares that mimicked the map's grid squares. Jeremy even handed me a long, skinny stick to use as a pointer so I could brief the entire sand table while standing up.

After the briefing, Jeremy told me I did a great job and offered me one of his meal, ready-to-eat (MRE) crackers. The offering of a cracker may seem insignificant today, but back in Ranger School it carried significant meaning. I was over six feet tall and came into the school at close to 220 pounds. When I finally graduated, I weighed 177. I knew Jeremy dipped, and I handed him a brand-new can of Copenhagen. After opening the can and putting almost half of it in his mouth, Jeremy told me he had just run out of tobacco and he anticipated our final three days of patrolling would be brutal without any dip. Over the next three days, I gave Jeremy the rest of my tobacco products, and he gave me whatever he didn't eat from his MREs.

Jeremy and I both passed our patrols and advanced to Mountain Phase. I can't remember the circumstances, but Jeremy, like many Ranger candidates, sustained an injury during mountaineering. As the rest of us headed out to the field, Jeremy and other injured Ranger students cleaned the barracks. On my way out, Jeremy said, "Check the second-floor trash can, under the liner." I dropped my ruck outside and ran back into the barracks to the second floor. I pulled out the liner and spotted an unopened Chili Mac MRE. Jeremy knew how to say goodbye. I figured I'd never see him again, and I appreciated him looking out for me when he had nothing to gain.

Less than two weeks later, I injured my shoulder falling off the side of a mountain while droning. Droning occurs when a sleep-deprived Ranger falls asleep while walking. At the time of my fall, I was carrying the M60 machine gun with the sling over my shoulder and a rucksack weighing over sixty pounds on my back. The next morning, I could not raise my left arm. Fortunately, a Ranger Instructor selected me to be platoon leader for the next mission. I felt so nervous that the pain went away. Even though adrenaline fueled me, my lack of mobility slowed me down. My frustration with my shoulder angered me and clouded my judgment. I failed my patrol and failed out of Ranger School.

Six months later, my shoulder healed enough for medical clearance and I returned to my second attempt at Ranger School. During the first day at Camp Rogers, while we dumped out all our gear for inspection, I noticed Jeremy had returned as well. By the time we got back to Mountain Phase, enough Rangers had failed out of the school that we were consolidated onto the same squad.

Jeremy and I were Ranger buddies until we both graduated. While there were other Ranger candidates who had transactional relationships trading tobacco for food and vice versa, going through hell is a lot better when you have a friend. Jeremy and I were not going to leave Fort Benning without our Ranger tabs—that was the mission. But we both understood the importance of having one another to rely on. Jeremy embodied the notion of looking out for someone else, and the lessons I learned from that relationship have never left me.

Ranger School graduation, Class 8-98

ORGANIZATIONAL BUDDY SYSTEM

Every organization needs a buddy system. It helps build culture and builds bonds between team members. At Berry Law, the buddy system serves as our top retention tool.

When we bring in a new team member, we will assign them a sponsor, similar to the way the military assigns a sponsor to new soldiers. Obviously, that sponsor needs to be a high performer so that the new team member learns what right looks like. The entire company needs to know that we commit to mentoring, training, and developing every new hire, and our sponsorship system solidifies that promise. Once the rest of the company understands our level of commitment to the new team member, they'll want to invest in the new team member as well.

This system works in the military, and it works in business.

During retention interviews, when asking team members why they stay at Berry Law, a common answer is the relationships with other team members. Longevity among team members has less to do with leadership, company mission, or pay than it does with the relationships they have built here. Paying your team above market value, giving them a purposeful mission, and showing them great leadership helps retain team members; but many companies boast those standards. If you can do those things and create a buddy system, you've positioned your team for even better retention results.

The feeling of safety and security at work from having a buddy who has their back enables team members to work swiftly and deliberately. We don't lose productivity to the drama manufactured by concerns that their job lacks the stability of a strong team.

At Berry Law, when we formally embraced the buddy system, we began to see that many of our best team players attracted other stars. Team members who had friends at other organizations recruited their buddies to work for us. I highly encouraged this type of recruiting. Imagine, your buddy from your previous company calls and wants to work with you. Who wouldn't want to work with their high-performing friends? Talent attracts talent, and work gets better when you can bring a highly talented person who you know, like, and trust to join your team.

When talent acquisition became a chokepoint to the growth of Berry Law, we recognized that almost everyone on the team had worked with someone who would be a perfect fit for our open positions. We encouraged employees to choose their team members. This worked especially well with our new CMO, Bob, who brought on an entire marketing team of top work buddies he had encountered over the decades of working at large ad agencies. Unfortunately, one team member saw this as an opportunity to do an underperforming buddy a favor. When we declined to hire this buddy, the team member felt slighted, but our rejection of the low performer reasserted the position and credibility of our leadership team.

To incentivize our hiring buddy system, we implemented Operation Spear Tip. Spear Tip serves as both a recruiting and a retention program. Here's how it works:

1. We offer a $25,000 recruiting bonus for any team member who recruits a buddy to join our team.

2. We pay out the bonus to the recruiting team member over a five-year period.

3. We pay the recruiting team member each year on the one-year anniversary of the new buddy's employment as long as both the buddy and the recruiting team member maintain full-time employment at Berry Law and neither the buddy nor the recruiting team member leaves the team for any reason.

Sure, we could pay headhunters to find talent, and we still do for top executives, but we found Spear Tip to be a less expensive and more effective way to secure new talent. Furthermore, the recruiting team member is highly incentivized to stay and ensure the success of the new team member.

In one example, one of our best attorneys recruited two paralegals for her team. So long as the paralegals stay for at least five years, that attorney will get $10,000 a year in recruitment bonuses for the next five years, totaling $50,000.

Not only does this tactic bring the buddy system of team building into our company at an expedited rate, but it also spreads positivity. In essence, the time and trust required to build teams can be compressed when our team recruits and hires the people we already know can perform based on firsthand experience. Yes, we still must vet the prospective team members, but our high performers are now incentivized to recruit their ideal players onto our team. As the saying goes, we are the sum of the five people we spend the most time with.

But wait, there's more! Spear Tip is also a retention and onboarding tool. The buddy system is crucial for onboarding new team members, and Spear Tip increases onboarding success and retention. Here's how: Remember the first day of school, when you didn't know anyone? You were nervous and self-conscious because you didn't know what to expect. With Spear Tip, our new team members come to Berry Law with a buddy they have known for years, someone they are comfortable asking the dumb questions, someone who they are excited to work with every day—an ally, a comrade, a trusted friend. The onboarding process becomes more immersive and less stressful. While Spear Tip does not replace our robust ninety-day onboarding program for new employees, it helps build working relationships faster.

When it comes to retention, studies show that people decide in the first ninety days whether they are going to stay at a company, and on average they decide within forty-four days according to a 2023 BambooHR study.[1] This same study shows that 93 percent of new hires want to shadow a colleague, 87 percent hope to make a friend at work, and 86 percent appreciate support from an onboarding buddy. Joining an organization where you already know at least one buddy usually means the new team member will feel like a member of the tribe sooner. A study in *Harvard Business Review* revealed Microsoft employees onboarded with a buddy were 23 percent more satisfied with their onboarding experience after the first week and 36 percent more satisfied at ninety days.[2]

When it comes to buddies, everything must come in pairs. As you scale your team, you will need built-in redundancies. I've often heard that growing companies never hire just one salesperson. Without a buddy or competitor in the office, the salesperson may never feel the excitement of competition. Buddy teams bring great energy to an organization. Beyond competition, even the best teams must deal with attrition. You don't want to have only one person with a skill set, you want a buddy team so that if you are ever down one person, you are never down a capability.

BEWARE THE BLUE FALCON

The opposite of a buddy is a Blue Falcon. The term "Blue Falcon" is the polite military code word for "Buddy Fucker." The Blue Falcon claims credit for the work of others, performs at a substandard level, shirks responsibility, and blames others for both personal and team failures. Sound familiar? Unfortunately, the Blue Falcon is not a mythical or rare creature. Blue Falcons exist in every organization, and you must not tolerate them. The survival of your team depends on it.

While we can all readily identify Blue Falcons in the military and in the civilian world, if we are being honest, we all display our own Blue Falcon shadow behavior from time to time. The key is awareness. In every action and communication, you are either a buddy or a Blue Falcon—you decide.

Are you claiming credit for your buddy's project? You are a Blue Falcon.

Did the project fail because you failed to do your part? You are a Blue Falcon.

Did the project not get done on time, not because you're too busy, as you claimed, but because you failed to manage your time? You are a Blue Falcon.

Did your lack of productivity result in your coworkers getting a smaller bonus? You are a Blue Falcon.

Did your vendor fail because you didn't adequately support them? You are a Blue Falcon.

So how do you avoid being a Blue Falcon?

Approach every project with this portion of the Ranger Creed: "I will shoulder more than my share of the task, whatever it may be." This is easier said than done.

We all have moments of weakness, and we all get overwhelmed. Sometimes, in the heat of the moment or in an exhausted state, we screw over a buddy, or worse, the entire team. When this happens, we need to accept responsibility, apologize, and move on. Every year I have moments where I blame someone else out loud and later realize the failure was my fault. I'd love to be able to say that, as a leader, I accept responsibility for everything on the spot, but sometimes it takes me a day or two to figure it out. When that happens, I apologize. The first step toward not being a Blue Falcon is recognizing when you are one.

If you fail to recognize the Blue Falcon in the room, it might be you. Richard Smith, former Equifax CEO, was in charge when the company experienced a historic data breach that made the personal financial history of 145.5 million Americans public. Smith's response was to blame the company and its protocols. He testified that a faulty scanner and one employee were responsible for the massive breach, passing the blame and not taking accountability for the huge mistake. Smith was smoked in a congressional inquest and later stepped down.[3]

Leaders never let Blue Falcons dictate the success or failure of a mission. When army vet Matthew Griffin started Combat Flip Flops, failure appeared at every turn. Their first factory created a shoddy product they had to give away. They found a second factory, but it shut down in the middle of production. "We made 4,000 pairs of flip flops in my garage to get the company going," he explains. "It was lots of hard work, but 'surrender' is not a Ranger word."[4] Griffin was let down by his major manufacturers, but he knew his company's success rested on his shoulders.

The buddy, the opposite of the Blue Falcon, cares more about whether they are carrying their share of the weight than whether someone else is performing. When things go wrong, the buddy points his thumb at his own chest and refuses to point his index finger at someone else. The true buddy knows that once he starts blaming others for the team's failure, he has given others all his power as a leader. The buddy never complains that he has the hardest job or that he works more hours than his peers. In fact, the buddy relishes the opportunity to contribute more to the team and mission.

Buddies always have your six—the six o'clock position behind your back. In the military, your buddy literally protects your blind side. As a civilian leader, my buddies protected my six even when I didn't want them to. As leaders, we can become so focused on one singular aspect of the mission that we need our buddies to set us straight. The greatest threat to our success is not our competitors, innovations, or regulations, but ourselves.

My general counsel, a former marine infantry officer with over thirty years of legal experience, cautioned me about risks, even when I didn't want to hear about them. He thought through the secondary and tertiary effects of all the team actions and often pulled me aside before or after meetings to confirm I understood the risks of action and inaction. While at times it seemed he was an obstacle, a walking risk assessment, and the rust that slowed the machine, his advice was invaluable. Had he cared more about his career or his ego than the team or the mission, he would have been more inclined to let me take unnecessary risks.

My CFO functions in the same way. He meticulously monitors our budget and our cash position. He's the buddy who urges me to not make stupid financial decisions. Leaders never see a shortage of opportunities, and while you can drown in opportunity, it's more likely you will bleed out of cash first. A good CFO is like that wise senior officer who says, "I know the auto dealership off base has the Mustang convertible you want, but paying 18 percent interest and half of your paycheck each month to buy it may be the stupidest thing you ever do."

I tend to fall in love with people who apply for our team, especially veterans. If I conducted every job interview, I'd probably hire 95 percent of applicants. I get fired up when someone expresses interest in us. Before I know it, I'm selling them on joining the team and selling myself on hiring them. Fortunately, my HRO buddy makes sure that we follow a hiring process that includes conducting background checks, calling references, and all the other best practices that I lack the patience to perform. It's like the first sergeant telling the private to not get married to the person he met last weekend. I know I need a buddy to slow down the process and ensure we are hiring the best candidates, rather than all the candidates.

CHOOSE YOUR BUDDY WISELY

In boot camp or basic training, the drill sergeant assigns you a "battle buddy," but as you progress in your military career, you get to choose your buddies. You may not get to choose your assignment, position, or duty station, but you choose the people you admire and the people you want on your team. Of course, in the military you don't always get to pick your team, but you get to pick who you trust within that team. Confucius said, "Have no friends not equal to yourself."[5] Choose a buddy who makes you better, not worse. More importantly, choose a buddy who has skills or abilities that you lack. My buddy is better than me at _____. If you can't complete the statement, you've got the wrong buddy. Maybe it's a skill or a character trait, but you lack it, and you need it to build a great team. The buddy game is won in the draft. Choose the right person, and you will become a champion. Choose the wrong person, and you will lose. When choosing a buddy, you are choosing a leader who will either expand your capabilities or detract from them.

We've all drafted buddies with promising futures only to be disappointed. Maybe they don't have the potential we anticipated. Maybe they lack the skill we believed they had. Sometimes we draft the buddy with amazing skills only to suffer because of their hidden character flaws.

While you never outgrow the buddy system, unfortunately, you will occasionally outgrow your buddies. I'm not talking about your high school friends or your drinking buddies at the bar whom you left behind to pursue a bigger life. I am talking about the professionals with whom you developed strong working relationships. When assigned a position that requires you to develop more skills and take on more responsibility, you need to find a buddy who levels up to that role.

As a platoon leader, my buddy was the platoon sergeant. My platoon sergeant not only managed the logistics in all the operations we planned but also kept his eye on me. The platoon sergeant inspected my uniform, critiqued my operations orders, and gave me feedback on my performance. When I became a company commander, my buddy was the first sergeant (1SG). The first sergeant let me know how my decisions were affecting our junior enlisted soldiers, which leaders I could trust, and most importantly, he held me accountable to the company standards that I set. Every new command position meant a new buddy with higher standards and higher expectations of me. To an officer, this means that your platoon sergeant may be a great platoon sergeant but might not be 1SG material. Fortunately, the army's management of personnel makes it highly improbable that a platoon leader and platoon sergeant duo will serve together as company commander and 1SG.

All leaders need buddies. Collaborative leaders are more affable, more respected, and more effective. Military green tab slots are often "lonely at the top" as a result of the hierarchical structure. In the business world, smart leaders make collaborative decisions as a part of a leadership team, when time allows. Your buddy team may be several members of your C-suite.

Just like the military, in the civilian world when you receive a promotion, it comes with a higher-level peer group. If you own a small business, your most important buddy could be your business partner or your executive assistant. The buddy can hold you accountable to your goals, protect your time, protect you from the poor decisions of others, and most importantly, protect you from your own bad judgment from time to time.

One of my most important hires as a leader of a company is my executive assistant. The executive assistant not only runs my day-to-day but holds me accountable and makes sure I am spending my time only on projects and relationships that I have previously designated will have a large impact on the growth of our organization. The executive assistant ensures that I spend my days focused on making decisions that improve the company rather than digging through daily minutia. In essence, my assistant is my force multiplier. The executive assistant functions similarly to the general officer's aide de camp who ensures that the general receives timely information, appears highly competent, and makes an impact wherever he goes.

The other important buddy team is the CEO-COO relationship. The chief operating officer (COO), like the military executive officer (XO) or deputy commander, is the second in command. This buddy team has a crucial dynamic. The COO must be strong where the CEO is weak and vice versa. When the CEO is center stage, the COO is backstage making it happen, unless their roles are reversed. The CEO-COO buddy team must maintain a unified front even though they focus on different aspects of the organization and may often disagree on the best course of action.

I recall countless military staff meetings where I would disagree with the commander's assessment or feel less than thrilled with a newly assigned mission. However, I knew that at the end of the meeting, I would brief my team with enthusiastic support for the commander's position, regardless of whether I agreed with it. The CEO-COO relationship must maintain the same level of alignment in the eyes of the team. This does not mean that they will always agree on everything. It means the company must believe they agree on everything.

The expectation of loyalty and trust in the CEO-COO

relationship maintains the same standards as the battle buddy you had in basic training. The stakes are the same as well—if the CEO fails, the COO will likely suffer and vice versa. Of course, at this level, a failure means you will be paying in dollars rather than push-ups and extra duty.

At Berkshire Hathaway, Warren Buffett, a former member of the Nebraska National Guard, and his COO Charlie Munger produced the most remarkable extended performance for investors ever recorded. At Facebook, Mark Zuckerberg focused on the product as well as strategic acquisitions, while Sheryl Sandberg focused on the business of Facebook and led its massive ad-sales endeavors.

A BUDDY TO PROTECT TIME AND REPUTATION

I know the CEO of a nine-figure company who never takes a meeting without his assistant or a member of his C-suite present. He relies on that buddy to not only protect his time but ensure that nothing gets miscommunicated or misinterpreted during his meetings. When I first heard him talk about having a buddy present for all communications, I thought he was arrogant and paranoid. My initial reaction was that leaders should be approachable to get meaningful feedback.

Experience has proven him right. I have found that when a junior team member wants to meet with the CEO for a one-on-one, there is a risk that during that meeting the junior team member will hear only what they want to hear. And, once they leave the meeting, everything they "heard" will be disseminated to the rest of the team as something you said. To avoid any miscommunication, I try to do two things:

1. At the end of the meeting, I ask the junior team member to "tell me what you just heard me say."

2. I have a buddy present to ensure everyone is on the same page and clear up any potential miscommunication.

As the leader, your job is to ensure clarity in all communications. You may not be speaking the same language as your junior team members because of knowledge gaps, generational differences, or blind spots you developed from the bright spotlight of leadership.

SPOUSE AS BUDDY

The most important buddy will be your spouse, so choose wisely. While many soldiers believe that if the army wanted them to have a spouse, they would have issued them one, a life partner may become the biggest reason for your successes or failures. If you intend to grow into something great, you need a buddy who is willing to grow with you.

I'm not suggesting you must work with your spouse, but I've seen more careers and businesses fall apart because of a person picking the wrong life partner than just about any other reason. If you can't count on your spouse to be the buddy to support you, don't get married; get a dog.

Of course, even if your spouse does not work in your company, you can gain a lot when you are both driven with shared goals. Robert Solano, army aviation officer, West Point graduate, and author of *Alpha Couples*, once told me that when he flew Blackhawks in Iraq and Afghanistan, "You never flew a one-ship mission. You always have a wingman to cover your six."[6] He explains that today, his wife Zaira, a highly successful businesswoman who owns several law firms, serves as his wingman. Zaira always has his back but doesn't hesitate to give him feedback. Zaira also helps him work on his self-identified shortcomings in a productive manner so that he can be a better buddy to her.

"The most important decision you make in life is who you choose to spend the rest of your life with," Solano says. He stresses the importance of alignment, especially when it comes to individual goals and values. Even though Solano and his wife work in different industries, they attend each other's workshops and conferences whenever possible. "Bring your spouse as your buddy so you can better support each other and run important decisions by each other. Your most important team member needs to understand what you are doing in order to help you."

The right buddy will support you, challenge you, and help you gain deeper insight into your own decision-making. As Solano points out, "Your first sergeant knows the organization well, and the first sergeant knows your shortcomings, but your first sergeant probably doesn't know what drives you. Your spouse knows you better than you know yourself." Solano appreciates the feedback his wife gives him, which is usually followed by, "But you're probably going to do X instead of what I just told you." This insight helps Solano approach a problem differently, and her advice helps him reach goals faster because she can spot the obstacles in his own behavior that he doesn't always recognize on his own.

The true buddy not only provides honest feedback and guidance but also inspires us to be a better buddy. G. K. Chesterton, one of the greatest and most prolific English writers of the twentieth century, said, "A real soldier does not fight because he has something that he hates in front of him. He fights because he has something that he loves behind his back."[7] We have often heard that when experiencing hell, the soldier fighting in the moment cares less about the mission, the constitution, or a piece of ribbon than he does about his brother next to him, whose life he must protect to save his own.

I'll admit, you can't create the same camaraderie in your civilian company that you had in the military. I have tried for years. Those of us who deployed together, suffered together, felt the highest of highs together and the lowest of lows together, have a bond that you won't find in any other organization than the United States military. The best we can do as veterans is hire other veterans and people who really want to live like heroes, develop other heroes, and die with the honor of knowing they gave all they had every single day to a worthwhile mission with a team they admired and respected. This all starts with taking care of your buddy.

AFTER-ACTION REVIEW ====

Sustain

1. You can't do all of it if you do it alone—not in the military and not in a growing organization.

2. A buddy team starts day one with onboarding.

3. Buddy teams can be a force multiplier in recruiting and retention.

Improve

1. You will outgrow some of your most proficient buddies.

2. If your buddy sucks the energy out of you, you have the wrong buddy.

3. If your buddy isn't better than you at something, find a new buddy.

3

MOVE WITH A SENSE
OF URGENCY

*Move fast. A sense of urgency is the one thing you can develop
that will separate you from everyone else.*

—Attributed to Brian Tracy

In the military, we move with a fierce sense of urgency that
propels us to do more than we believed possible. In a training
environment, we run everywhere and manage our time on a
training schedule that forces us to move with deliberate haste.
We start on time, and we end on time. Drill instructors teach
us to either move with a sense of purpose or find ourselves
left behind.

Speed wins. We run to chow, we run to the classroom, we
run to and from the barracks. "Double-time" means run. It's
the term your platoon sergeant used when they told you they
wanted something done quickly—when they needed you to

move fast. It's called double-time because you are doubling the speed at which your feet hit the pavement.

The opposite of double-time is not "halt!" but rather a slow meander, just existing. Every day we live without urgency we get slower, fatter, and less motivated. Some veterans, and soldiers on leave, get caught up in the freedoms of civilian life, drinking excessively, eating junk, and developing lazy habits resulting in poor health. I've met severely disabled combat veterans who live much better, healthier lives than veterans with no disabilities who, without a sense of urgency or purpose, slowly kill themselves.

Years ago, as a civilian lawyer in my neatly pressed suit and tie, I dug my heels into the cement sidewalk as I trekked to the courthouse at a fast pace. While others around me strolled at leisurely speeds, I weaved in and out of the foot traffic around me. I had somewhere to be. "Where's the fire?" an older lawyer asked as I passed him by. I responded with some polite, meaningless drivel.

Yet inside, I was shaking my head. I could tell that this man's fire in life was all but extinguished. He had no apparent desire to use his time efficiently. And instead of gaining motivation from my speed, he discouraged my actions. Interactions like these satisfy me because I know I am not falling into the trap of complacency most fall into as they go about life and become more comfortable.

For veterans, this transition often takes place when we separate from the military and enter an entirely new world. No longer are first sergeants and drill instructors pressuring us to move quickly. Those screaming voices around us disappear and the pace slows.

Never lose the desire to run everywhere. It's what separates us from those who have never had anything worth running to protect or anything to chase. After we depart from our last duty station with DD-214 in hand, we find ourselves surrounded by people who perpetually choose the easiest journeys. They get lazier and lazier at every fork in the road and suggest we do the same. Our sense of urgency is our competitive advantage in life. Move with a purpose, move with urgency, or move out of the way.

The next time you're out in a densely populated public area, observe the people around you. Notice that most of them aren't hustling from one location to another. They're simply hobbling along, head down, not paying attention to what's around them. They demonstrate zero situational awareness, and they become offended when someone passes them. As a person who used to get road rage in grocery store aisles, I now feel a pang of sympathy when trying to pass those hopeless souls.

Need a bit of help getting back on track after a long separation from the military? It's okay if you do. Remember, civilian life in America isn't built on the need to run everywhere. So if you find yourself needing a push, envision your drill sergeant standing beside you, shouting in your ear.

Remember those days? Do you remember the motivation manufactured by that brimmed hat bouncing up and down beside you, pushing you to keep pace for fear of the pain that would come if you didn't? Go through life with that feeling and see how quickly you break away from the crowd of lethargic civilians and into a highly productive lifestyle.

When you're the new person at a company, all eyes are on you. Everyone is paying attention to how you act. And while you may not be able to contribute to the organization immediately, everyone recognizes hustle. Those who show up in the morning early and move quickly, work diligently, and keep their minds moving are the ones who will rise in the ranks faster than their peers. As a brand-new second lieutenant, I couldn't hide my inexperience. However, I knew I controlled my appearance, my level of physical fitness, my attitude, and my work ethic. I tried to show up like a leader, even though I didn't know how to lead. It worked.

We all know what it looks like when people run everywhere. They earn respect. They demand respect and they get it—and admiration, too—based on their actions. They move with the sense of purpose we all wish we had. Their hyper-responsive communications and speedy task execution generate trust from their peers, supervisors, and subordinates.

We control the rate of our forward progress. In the infantry, we know we have to fight for every inch of terrain. We know that if we reach the objective before the enemy, we seize the terrain without a fight; now the enemy must fight for every inch. Run fast: it's a lot easier to be first and go on the defensive than to go on the offensive. Move with a sense of purpose. Get there first. Seize the terrain.

Of course, your hustle will earn you a reputation, and the less driven will criticize you. Nonperformers hate achievers.

Achievers make nonperformers feel threatened by exposing their incompetence or laziness. You must never apologize for raising the standard. If a coworker tells you that you are working too hard, that you're making everyone else look bad or you need to slow down, you just found your enemy. If you maintain your hustle, that person will either improve and get on your level or try to sabotage you. As a leader, your goal is to get everyone to perform at a higher tempo and intensity.

All the garrison training hustle not only gets us in great physical shape but prepares our minds for combat training. The Operations Order (OPORD) is a plan to complete a mission. Every mission has a deadline by which the mission must be completed. From the deadline, we conduct backward planning to ensure we accomplish every phase of the mission on time. Time is of the essence because we must synchronize our actions with adjacent units and friendly forces who assist us in completing our mission.

We must cross the line of departure on time so that our headquarters knows we have left their area of operations. We must pass through friendly forces boundaries on time to avoid fratricide. We must reach our objective on time to coordinate firepower. We must complete our actions on the objective on time to advance to safety before enemy reinforcements arrive or enemy artillery begins raining from the sky.

We complete the entire mission with a sense of urgency because missing a "time hack" could compromise the entire mission.

Just like in the military, in business, time is of the essence. Just as at the rifle qualification range targets pop up for a brief second before they mechanically drop, most opportunities are time sensitive. "I'm up, he sees me, I'm down." Without a sense of urgency, we miss the target without even sending lead downrange.

POTENTIAL CLIENTS MOVE FASTER THAN POP-UP TARGETS

Research shows that customer contacts expect hyper-responsiveness. While consumers give you a little more time than the three seconds per target you get at the pop-up range, they expect immediate contact. If a potential new customer calls and you don't engage, they will call somebody else. If the potential customer reaches out to you on social media and you do not immediately respond, they will contact someone else. If the live chat on your website does not respond automatically, they will navigate somewhere else.

A 2021 HubSpot survey revealed that 90 percent of customers rate an "immediate" response as important or very important when they have a customer service question.[1] Sixty percent of customers define "immediate" as ten minutes or less. According to a 2023 study done by Gorgias, approximately 66 percent of customers expect an immediate response to their inquiries, creating a growing trend in consumer reliance on chatbots to resolve their issues.[2] According to research by *Forbes Advisor*, website visitors in 2024 typically spend an average of only fifty-four seconds on a single page, which means leveraging a chat agent to keep a customer engaged with an immediate response is more likely to lead to higher sales conversions and repeat site visitors.[3]

A pain point caused the consumer to call, and they want it resolved now. Think about calling the doctor. By the time you call the doctor, you know it's serious and you are willing to travel to the doctor's office and maybe even make a co-pay payment. Consumers want the problem solved now. This is great if your sales team moves with a sense of urgency. This is bad news if you think you are so special that the consumer will wait for your team to return their calls. You're wrong.

Time kills all deals. The potential customer who wants to immediately execute a contract today may change his mind tomorrow. Why? Conditions change, emotions change, value changes, and financial circumstances change—quickly. Conduct due diligence, but just as your customers want to hire now, your partners should want to close the deal today.

Anadarko Petroleum lost its chance at a $33 billion deal from Fortune 500 company, Chevron. Chevron decided to walk away from the deal after Anadarko entertained a bid from another oil and gas giant, creating a bidding war that was taking longer than Chevron wanted to wait. Before Anadarko could strike a deal, Chevron pulled out and focused on returning value to its shareholders and investing in other opportunities.

While indecision and unnecessary slow movement cause failure in both military operations and business, when someone is too eager to make a deal, beware. If your sense of urgency gets the best of you, you may enter into a bad deal with a vendor, or worse, a new business partner. Knowing that time kills all deals, temper your sense of urgency with a process for analyzing new opportunities that streamline your actions so as not to kill the deal while ensuring you are doing proper due diligence.

One of the lessons the army teaches in training for optimal performance is that "slow is smooth and smooth is fast." In business, intentionally slowing down a deal can actually get it done faster than moving so quickly that you create a lot of friction with banks, lenders, partners, or other decision-makers.

Understanding how to harness the power of your sense of urgency takes time because you must develop the skill of judgment. Notice I chose the word develop rather than master. If we could master the skill of judgment, we would stop making bad decisions. The skilled leaders whose judgment I trust most still make bad decisions from time to time. I make several bad decisions a week. However, through countless mistakes, I have learned to factor urgency into every decision.

While the army emphasizes the importance of decisive leaders who take bold initiatives, it discourages hasty decisions that fail to calculate risk. As the leader of your organization, some of the biggest risks will be in hiring the wrong team members and failing to move quickly enough to secure great talent.

HIRE WITH A SENSE OF URGENCY

When your best future team members are available, pull the trigger. Your best candidates never look for jobs because they are never unemployed. You must recruit them, and you must do so aggressively and with a sense of urgency. The cliché of slow to hire, fast to fire only makes sense when you don't personally know the candidates.

A lot of consultants will tell you to make these well-known, top-performing candidates jump through hoops like every other candidate. But top performers who you have been recruiting for years are not like every other candidate. Would you rather strike out from watching pitches or from taking swings and missing? Would you rather accelerate the hiring process for a known performer and get burned or move too slowly and watch a competitor hire the perfect person for your team? Personality tests, cover letters, background checks, and references never tell you everything you need to know. Sometimes you're better off hiring, being wrong, and learning from the mis-hire than not hiring at all because you lacked the guts to move with a sense of urgency.

Top performers are always in high demand and tend to be employed most of the time. A 2023 McKinsey and Company article states that only 4 percent of an average organization consists of "thriving stars," defined as "super engaged workers who not only perform at high levels themselves but also appear to spread their positive engagement and commitment to others."[4] Many top performers are not actively looking for new job opportunities but are open to considering them if approached. LinkedIn's Hiring Statistics for 2022 revealed that around 70 percent of the global workforce consists of passive candidates, with 15 percent being completely satisfied and not considering a change.[5] The same study found that 62 percent of talent teams find more high-quality candidates through sourcing than from inbound applications.

In 2022, the Department of Defense reported that only 23 percent of Americans ages seventeen to twenty-four are qualified to serve without a waiver to join the military.[6] More problematic is that only 9 percent of those eligible to serve would even consider it.

In hiring, if you don't move with a sense of urgency, you can get so far behind that you must lower your standards to keep the business going. Today's military recruiters have experienced this firsthand with the difficulty in finding qualified recruits and then asking the military to reduce standards to get enough qualified candidates. This happens cyclically. The military ramps up for a major conflict and must quickly fill its ranks with qualified service members.

Back in the days of the draft, a large, mandatory candidate pool put the military in a better position to maintain its standards. Back then, the military also maintained lower standards. Judges commonly encouraged young men convicted of crimes to join the military: "Go to war or go to jail." Today's military rarely allows men and women with criminal convictions to enter service without a waiver. The standards are even higher for recruiting officers. I remember requesting a waiver for an officer candidate school applicant who received a citation from a game warden for not having enough life jackets in his motorboat. This talented leader almost didn't become an officer because some bureaucrat O-6 didn't have time to sign the waiver.

Now, without a draft, when the military "ramps up," enlistment bonuses abound. Consider this: With its massive budget and reputation for creating leaders, even the greatest military force in the history of the world faces challenges in recruiting top performers. Whether you have a team of one or one hundred thousand, you don't have the budget or the prestige of the United States military and thus, when you know you have the opportunity to hire a high performer on the spot, you may want to move with a sense of urgency.

CONTRIVED URGENCY

While you must operate with a sense of urgency, you must also be able to identify a false sense of urgency. When you hear a salesperson tell you that an opportunity is only available for a "limited time," your BS detector should pick up on the inflated sense of urgency. While some offers do have time limits for good reason, time limits are often sales gimmicks. These gimmicks are not only effective but sometimes necessary to get indecisive consumers to purchase an item or service that will vastly improve their lives.

Another example of contrived urgency is when vendors use a false premise of scarcity to create FOMO (fear of missing out)—that because of "limited supply," you must buy "now or never." Sometimes supplies really are limited by supply chains, manufacturing constraints, or shortage of qualified team members. But if a company is bombarding you with marketing about their "limited supply," they are bombarding others. Logic tells us that if they are spending money to tell everyone that supply is limited, it is not.

Contrast this with the car dealership outside of every military base where the dealer just sold Private Snuffy the one-of-a-kind, bright green 1999 Honda Civic with gold rims for just $15,000 on a 19 percent interest payment plan. While Snuffy bought a unique and limited item, that doesn't mean he got a good deal or that he made a financially responsible decision. If your sense of urgency comes from FOMO, halt and think through whether their claim of limited supplies or services makes sense. Do a little research and you may discover this company has miraculously been operating with "limited supplies" for years.

Think back to the hungriest, most desperate salesperson you've ever met. At what point did the desperation erode your trust in the product or salesperson? It seems that the overwhelming advice from sales trainers is to contact a prospect several times a day by telephone, email, and social media until you get the sale. They tell you that the consumer has so much going on in their lives that they need constant reminders that they need to buy your product or service in case they forget. However, their actions come off more akin to a teenager asking to borrow the car several times a day. At some point the consumer recognizes the salesperson's sense of urgency is not about a reminder but rather an attempt to beat them into submission.

FADING URGENCY AND A FADING WILL TO WIN

Now reverse the facts. Not enough follow-up can result in distrust as well. I recently set a timeline and decision-making process to hire a vendor for a new marketing campaign. After weeks of conducting research and speaking to customers of the vendors, I narrowed my decision to my top two vendors. While I didn't conduct the full MDMP (military decision-making process) or produce a DECMAT (decision matrix), my research led me to believe that both vendors possessed the capabilities to achieve my intent. Vendor A had a superior product, but Vendor B demonstrated superior strategy and delivery systems. If I chose Vendor A, I might have a great campaign that no one would ever see. If I chose Vendor B, the campaign would be good enough to meet my intent and widely distributed.

My sense of urgency kept me on a tight timeline for the project. I calendared a date to make the decision. After scrutinizing the scope of work for each project, I sent out one final email making my intent crystal clear with my final RFI (request for information) seven days prior to my decision deadline. Vendor A responded that her team would get me an answer within twenty-four hours. The email I sent to Vendor B triggered an auto-response out-of-office email, and no one from Vendor B's team followed up for seven days.

As I pondered the importance of the project, I could not stand the thought of Vendor B not responding or having a system in place to ensure their team stayed in close contact with their clients. Either Vendor B lacked interest in my project, or Vendor B lacked the systems to deliver. If they lacked the initiative and systems to close the sale, I had no confidence they would be able to execute their superior strategy and delivery plan. I chose Vendor A.

A CULTURE OF URGENCY

A sense of urgency becomes part of company culture when you systematize hyper-responsive communications. While sales teams must never morph into a gang of pushy stalkers, statistics tell us that follow-up is key to a great sales process. However, "urgent" and "often" are two different objectives. While the sales team should urgently follow up, a follow-up that is too frequent appears pushy and desperate. What is the right amount of follow-up? That is a question of frequency rather than urgency. Frequency can be tested and measured until it is optimized. How soon should I follow up? Immediately. When immediate follow-up is not possible, follow up no later than twenty-four hours after the initial contact.

Why twenty-four hours or less? Because everything in our firm's culture of urgency requires a response in twenty-four hours. If a client reaches out, we respond in twenty-four hours or less. If a team member reaches out to a peer, we respond in twenty-four hours. If a subordinate reaches out to a supervisor, they get a response in twenty-four hours. Even at the directorate level, responses occur in less than twenty-four hours. The rapid response requirement goes both up and down the chain of command.

But what if I can't get the information so I can fully and accurately respond in twenty-four hours? Respond in less than twenty-four hours regardless of whether you have the problem solved. When servicing your customers and clients, always respond with a sense of urgency. I tell my team to return the calls the same day, even if you don't have a solid answer. Be transparent, tell the client you do not yet have complete answers to their questions, but that you wanted to give them the respect and courtesy of responding to their call the same day.

In your team's culture, when team members are slow to respond, they can appear arrogant, apathetic, or even passive-aggressive. The person who made the effort to send the message and does not get a response for days often feels rejected, unappreciated, and ignored. Respond with urgency whether it's a client, customer, subordinate, peer, supervisor, collaborator, or significant other. You don't need to wait until you have the problem solved, but you do need to acknowledge, validate, and respect their effort to communicate with you. Move with a sense of urgency in your research, decisions, and communications. This does not mean you rush to failure. On the contrary, you act deliberately and take action to make informed decisions. What you don't do is move so slowly that you find yourself stuck with default options because your competitor who moved with a sense of urgency got the opportunity that you squandered.

AFTER-ACTION REVIEW

Sustain

1. Customers and team members expect hyper-responsiveness.

2. Time kills all deals.

3. As General George S. Patton said, "A good plan violently executed *now* is better than a perfect plan next week."[7]

Improve

1. Slow is smooth, and smooth is fast; systems make your organization smooth.

2. If a vendor or potential partner presses too hard to go too fast, proceed with caution.

3. The need for speed never absolves you from failing to conduct due diligence.

4

HURRY UP AND WAIT: THE ART OF STRATEGIC, OPERATIONAL, AND TACTICAL PATIENCE

Luck is what happens when preparation meets opportunity.

—Attributed to Seneca

R eady . . .
　　Set . . .
Wait.

First Sergeant Fowler always seemed hurried. The fierce sense of urgency dripped from his face in beads of sweat. His voice reverberated throughout the company area—loud commands rapidly fired from his mouth between puffs from a cigarette. He walked with such a sense of purpose that if anyone other than the company commander walked in front of him, 1SG Fowler would leave boot prints on their backs without slowing down. It didn't matter if we were doing physical training (PT) at 0530 or we had just completed the final formation for the day, 1SG Fowler was in a hurry to get where he was going, and he expected you to be in a hurry too. During our weekly company five-mile run, 1SG Fowler usually finished first. I never understood how this man could smoke like a chimney and run like the wind. He could smoke a cigarette in less than one minute and run a mile in under six.

If you served in the military, you're all too familiar with the phrase "hurry up and wait." From the day you show up at basic

1SG Mike Fowler supervising the Grim Reapers in a tug-of-war competition against another company

training or boot camp until the day you retire from the military, your career revolves around this concept.

Run to the chow hall to wait in line. Get to formation ten minutes early just to wait in formation for another ten minutes. Get to the firing range before daylight and then sit through hours of safety briefs and wait your turn to fire your weapon. Then wait around the rest of the day until everyone is finished and move at light speed to polish up the brass and pick up cigarette butts before the sun sets.

If you served, you know that the primary focus of every move you make is readiness and preparedness so that you can take the fight to the enemy. But seizing the initiative requires a lot of waiting, until it's time to move with a purpose.

The first sergeant's emphasis on timeliness and preparation paid off. In March of 1999, we arrived in Bosnia a week prior to the bombings in Kosovo. Everything ramped up quickly—and then the lull. Most of us expect our first deployment to be full of action and excitement, but we quickly learn that deployments maintain the same hurry-up-and-wait cycle as training.

If you've never deployed, you probably wonder why soldiers do so much stupid stuff on deployments, from hitting chem-light-soaked golf balls off the tops of bunkers at night, to penning crude jokes on every porta potty, to off-roading in the desert to see whether a Humvee could catch air on a sand dune. Most of it happens during the lull, the downtime that takes place after moments of intense excitement, when boredom sets in.

In our case, the first sergeant creatively found ways to create urgency where none needed to exist to stop us from doing stupid

In Bosnia on another hurry-up-and-wait mission

stuff. When the time came to move like lightning, we did. A few months into the deployment, the task force commander called me into the TOC (tactical operations center), pointed at a map on the wall, and asked me, "How quickly can you get your platoon to this checkpoint?" My company commander had identified a target of opportunity in our area of operations several weeks prior, and now the division wanted to exploit the opportunity. The task force commander wanted to show the division what we could do.

"At fifty kilometers per hour, we can get there in about thirty-five minutes," I responded. My company commander nodded in approval.

"That's not the question I asked you," the task force commander fired back. "How quickly can you get there?"

It took me a second to realize he was really asking me to brief him on the status of my platoon's readiness. How long would it take us to load up our Humvees, arm our weapons systems, roll out of the gate, and reach the objective driving as fast as we could?

"We're ready to move now. Once we get out of the gate, we can get there in twenty-four minutes," I lied.

First Sergeant Fowler, who was quietly standing in the back of the room, quickly slipped out. Before I left the meeting, the first sergeant had rounded up my platoon sergeant and a couple of my squad leaders. The drivers conducted preventive maintenance checks and services (PMCS) and then removed drip pans and chock blocks. Our vehicles moved toward the front gate. The platoon sergeant staged the vehicles and conducted precombat inspections and radio checks before I made it to the staging area to brief the platoon. It was that reputation for preparedness that earned us the opportunity to set outer-ring security for a critical mission to extract a suspected war criminal. No more sitting around, or at least not for the next eight hours.

At the conclusion of my brief, we loaded into the Humvees, requested permission to leave from HQ, exited the gate, and quickly advanced to our checkpoint. We set the outer security perimeter and, as soon as we did, we heard the helicopters chopping air overhead and the rumbling of Humvees accelerating toward our position—we arrived just in time.

During the mission, we demonstrated our agility to mount up and move—1SG Fowler had expected this performance. As a young lieutenant, I mistakenly believed he wanted us to get the best missions, so he wanted us to be prepared for the opportunity. Later, I learned his real concern had more to do with our survival in deployments to come. Complacency kills. Lack of preparation kills.

HURRY TO BE READY IN BUSINESS

As briefly explained in the preceding chapter, some of those biggest missed opportunities came in the form of missed hires. It's always better to hurry up and wait for the right prospective employee than to hire late. We now try to hire the talent before we are ready.

At Berry Law, we reached a point where we knew the business would not scale without robust internal technology capabilities. We knew that an in-house chief information officer (CIO) would be expensive but a key investment in our growth and our future. We also knew we had no idea what to do with a CIO after we hired him. After we committed to hiring our first in-house CIO, the best candidate serendipitously walked in through our front door five days prior to our formal search. We hired a headhunter, and at her suggestion we began fine-tuning our candidate job description—which didn't exist. Had I been moving with a sense of urgency I would have offered the guy the job within a few days. However, we were still researching salaries and other administrative minutia. By the time we invited the candidate for a formal interview ten days later, he had already accepted a position in another industry. It took us another year to find a qualified candidate. We lost momentum, morale, and money because we were not prepared with a clear vision and role for our CIO.

In hindsight, had we created a long-range plan and forecasted our needs, we could have determined the exact window by which we would need the CIO. Leaning forward from that vantage point, we should have expeditiously created an accurate job description and scripted the story of the perfect candidate long before the quarter in which we needed to hire. Because we failed to hurry and wait, the opportunity caught us flat-footed.

Author of *The Second in Command* and COO Alliance founder Cameron Herold later told me that hiring is like duck hunting. You need as many ducks as you can get. "Don't just repeat the same duck call, put out decoys, plan to bring in twenty if you want to hire one. Create excitement, build a crowd around the decoys. Don't pull the trigger until the ducks surround you. If you can't create a sense of urgency, excitement, and exclusivity around your new position, you will never close your best potential hires."[1]

So get up before dawn, get to your duck blind, put out the decoys, and wait for the ducks to come to you. And when they come, be ready.

Hurry up and plan, expect to wait until the opportunity arises, and then strike hard. We now always hurry up and wait. At Berry Law, we know what we will accomplish every quarter in our three-year plan and update it every ninety days. We know what we need, and when we get the opportunity to hire our next star, we strike fast and hard. We also approach hiring as an opportunity to level up. We never stop hiring top talent, even when we don't have room. We make space at the top.

Know who you need and when. Hire early; never hire late.

It's better to be ready and seize the best player than to get stuck with the leftovers when you need a warm body right now. I've never regretted an early hire, but I've regretted some late hires.

Because we aggressively hire veterans, former college athletes, and people who grew up with a strong work ethic like farm kids and paper carriers, we rarely pass when highly qualified stars serendipitously trip our radar. A couple of years ago, while at a court hearing with scores of lawyers, I noticed a professional-looking young man whose presence set him apart from the other lawyers. Surprisingly, this young man introduced himself to me as a law student. This former marine worked for another law firm as a student law clerk. I invited the marine to lunch that week to meet some of our team members. When I learned the marine ranked near the top of his class, we expedited him through our hiring funnel to hire him as a clerk for our team.

WHERE VETERANS EXCEL

As a civilian, you never know when you're going to get your next opportunity, but you need to be ready when it comes. Hurry up and wait taught you how to be prepared for those moments. It taught you how to execute at a time when others inevitably scramble. Business competitors appear in many forms, but they all have one thing in common: they hunt soft targets. They prey on the opportunities that the unprepared let slip.

Hurry up and wait remains our standard. Information gathered last month may be stale today because you failed to act on it. A hurry-up-and-wait attitude can buy planning time, additional analysis, and a head start. A hurry-up-and-wait culture doesn't slow you down, it allows you to take the initiative.

Most veterans joke about the stupidity of the hurry-up-and-wait mentality. I remember one morning at the National Training Center in Fort Irwin, California. We lined up every Bradley Fighting Vehicle in the battalion at 0430 just outside the motor pool, but we did not cross the line of departure (LD) until 0700. We missed a night's sleep for nothing, but that was part of the culture.

You probably remember from your earliest military experiences, standing in line at the Central Issue Facility (CIF) for hours to draw several duffel bags worth of gear, most of which you never used. Then, when you joined a "real" military unit, soldiers arrived at the company area before daybreak, completed the day's training, and then waited in the parking lot for hours for the end-of-the-day formation to be released to go home.

The first time hurry up and wait made sense to me was during field training to conduct an ambush. Conducting a deliberate ambush meant reviewing weeks of intel on enemy movement patterns, civilian traffic patterns, and the routines of any person or living thing near the kill zone. Once we learned when to expect enemy movement on the road at the same time and in the same direction they always traveled, we hurried to set the ambush. Using the terrain for cover and concealment, we strategically placed our weapons to mass our firepower at the exact location where the enemy would be most vulnerable. We waited for the enemy to arrive. After the enemy entered the kill zone, we patiently waited until the enemy reached the center of the kill zone before initiating contact with our most casualty-producing weapon. Then, and only then, did we initiate a symphony of superior firepower known as the "mad minute." The sound of Claymore mines, machine guns, and rifles harmoniously filled the air at the enemy's most vulnerable moment. Hurry up and wait for victory.

Later in my career, as a current operations officer on a division staff, I learned that hurry up and wait also meant exercising operational patience. Most veterans know about the warfighter exercise. This is the two-week, twenty-four/seven computer-simulated battle that serves as a report card for field grade officers but bores everyone else to tears.

During my first warfighter exercise, as a junior officer, I served as a "puckster," which meant I moved unit icons on a big screen map for two weeks straight on a twelve-hour-a-day shift. Later, as a field grade officer, I experienced the training differently. An army division has roughly ten thousand soldiers. As the day shift current operations officer, I reported to the chief of operations (CHOPS). As the computer-simulated battle raged on for two weeks, I watched on large screens as blue (friendly) and red (enemy) icons moved into position and listened to the radio chatter of multiple units engaged with the enemy. I suddenly longed for the boredom I had felt as a puckster. In my role as a field grade officer, I incessantly managed chaos.

I recall seeing elements of an enemy division enveloping a friendly infantry battalion. I grabbed the radio and told the infantry battalion HQ they needed to move *now*, or they would be slaughtered. An hour later, after chasing other rabbits, I looked at the screen and the doomed infantry battalion had not moved. I panicked—the battalion had failed to move and now it was too late. A senior captain who observed my distress sat back in his chair and said, "Major, they sealed their fate long before you called them. You need to exercise some operational patience; the icons on the screen don't move when you tell them to move. A battalion cannot move that fast."

The important lesson I learned throughout that two-week exercise was that the larger the organization, the longer it takes to initiate movement. Hurry up and wait is absolutely necessary to scale any organization. By the time information comes from the top to those with boots on the ground, it may be too late to take action. The army has a one-third/two-thirds rule that says, as a leader, you only spend one-third of the allotted time planning so that your subordinate units have two-thirds of the remaining time to complete their plan. We issue a warning order to initiate the movement of our subordinate teams so they can begin their parallel planning process and start necessary movement long before our plan is complete.

As a civilian I have found that the larger our organization grows, the more important the one-third/two-thirds rule becomes. Bigger means not only less agile but slower.

But how can you afford to wait when time is of the essence? In an advertising world full of hype, we hear that to be successful in business, you either have to be the first, or be the best. The truth is, being the best takes time. What about being first? Many times, the first into the market is the first to be slaughtered. Sometimes the public is not ready for a new product or service. More often, the company that rolled it out lacked the resources to see the plan all the way through. Yes, success requires moving with a fierce sense of urgency, and many times that means moving faster than competitors, but it also means moving deliberately and showing operational patience from time to time.

More than once, I have launched a marketing campaign before I had an adequate sales or intake team in place. I became so excited about the marketing campaign that I underestimated its success and failed to evaluate the capacity of our sales team. The first time I did this, I believed we did not have enough intake people in place, so I doubled the number of team members answering phones and responding to webforms. Nonetheless, within forty-eight hours of launching the campaign we were dropping over 50 percent of our calls, fielding complaints, and noticing a spike in negative reviews and feedback.

When we halted the campaign to catch up, the psychological damage was done. The entire company believed we now had more leads than we could handle for eternity. We suffered from lead obesity. Our sales team claimed the plentiful leads drowned them, but they really just got complacent. Now they could achieve their objectives without a sense of urgency. And to the detriment of our reputation, we failed to respond to almost a hundred incoming leads.

To fix the problem, I figured that I needed to gin up more urgency. For my next campaign, I hired a call center manager and built up the intake team. Two weeks after the campaign launched, it appeared to be a failure. Sales numbers were down almost 15 percent even though we had doubled our marketing spend on the new campaign. As we dug into the numbers, we validated that the marketing campaign had generated several qualified leads. Next, we dug deep into our call center data.

The call center data shocked me. We were again dropping 50 percent of our calls. The call center manager indicated that we could not continue to live answer all the calls and told us we needed an "IVR," or interactive voice response—the automated phone system that prompts callers to choose menu options from which it can perform actions, such as provide prerecorded information or route calls so we could separate incoming potential clients from current clients. We hurried to implement the IVR. As I watched the call center data closely each day for the next week, I could not believe what I saw. Even with the IVR, we were dropping 50 percent of calls. Painfully, I later realized that all the calls we were dropping were coming to our sales team. Even though we believed we'd fixed our problem, we continued to bleed expensive leads. Hurrying to create the marketing campaign was not the flaw. The flaw came from my failure to exercise patience and wait until we had a solid intake team and plan in place to handle the leads we anticipated from the marketing strategy.

One of my recurring problems is that I get motivated to start a project, begin researching, and once I have something that I feel will be successful, I want to launch immediately. My sense of urgency may come from military training, excitement, or fear, but once I get into hurry mode, I struggle to throttle down to wait mode and get all the pieces in place before going on the offensive. I've counseled many young officers on tempering speed with prudence and tactical patience. We must remain mindful of the adage, "While the early bird catches the worm, the second mouse gets the cheese." Sometimes it's better to be methodical than fast, but we must always be ready to be fast.

GO EVERYWHERE EARLY AND PREPARED

The drill sergeant always made sure soldiers arrived early and prepared. When I arrived at my first unit, it was no different. The first sergeant issued a packing list for every training event. Whether we were ruck marching, taking the training bus, convoying in Humvees, or traveling in formation with our Bradleys, we always arrived early, which gave us time to prepare our gear and weapon systems while on site. On many occasions, we arrived at the training site early and spent time conducting hip-pocket training while waiting for instructors, observer controllers, or some other element. The first sergeant made it clear that when it was time to train or roll out of the gate during deployment, his company was always ready and would never be the reason a mission was delayed.

HURRY-UP-AND-WAIT PRESENTATIONS

Many veterans may also remember the hurry-up-and-wait mentality inside the air-conditioned classroom. As a new infantry lieutenant at Fort Benning (renamed Fort Moore), I remember the days spent in Building 4. Our entire class of over two hundred

2LTs was always present and accounted for ten minutes before the instructor walked in and we were called to our feet to stand at attention. Then we suffered hours of "death by PowerPoint" slides. Looking back, it's amazing how all those classes started on time and ended on time.

Much later, as a staff officer, I learned that starting on time and ending on time took a lot of hurry-up-and-wait skill. I lost weeks of my life creating and inspecting PowerPoint slides, rehearsing talking points, conducting technology rehearsals, and then running a timed rehearsal of the entire presentation to ensure it did not run too short or too long. Of course, even with all these precautions, we still ran into technology delays or other snags that made us appear unprepared from time to time. Sometimes even when you hurry up and wait, one miscalculation can make you appear unprepared.

The civilian application of hurry up and wait means superior preparedness: nobody wants to hire a company that does not do its homework. I've walked out of meetings where the other company comes unprepared; they just wasted my time. They proved no data, no plans, no value, just an idea. I am never going to hire vendors or candidates who cannot get technology to work on time or fail to start a sales brief or a remote conference call on time. Seriously, if you can't competently present your materials on time, why should I believe anything else you or your company does will be competent work? Perhaps this seems harsh, but either you pursue excellence or you don't. There is nothing less excellent than wasting someone's time because you failed to prepare.

THE COMPOUNDING EFFECT

The hurry-up-and-wait philosophy also favors those who put forth a strong, consistent effort. Efforts compound over time—some of my best business relationships came from colleagues who wanted to work together but our interests didn't quite align at the time. However, once our interests synced up, my knowledge of and trust in this person allowed us to work together quickly. Hurry up and be hyper-responsive to calls, texts, and emails. Let them know you value them by your actions. Prompt, courteous responses tell me that not only is the other person interested in me, but they share my drive and expectations. However, the key is to wait until the right time. You reach out not when you need a favor, but when you can be of value. The trust that you build by being prepared to serve compounds every year that they don't need your services.

Think about who gets your quick responses: your spouse, kids, close friends. When you hurry up to show interest, you treat that person like a close friend. People do business with people they know, like, and trust. I like hyper-responsive people because they make me feel like they value my time. I also feel like they "get me"—it's like I know them. Finally, I trust them because they treat me like I'm a priority, and I can count on them for a quick response.

However, I remain skeptical of businesses that flaunt their hustle but lack proof of results. It's as if they spend all their time cultivating relationships and opportunities rather than delivering what they promise. Wait until you have results before you blow up your prospect's phone promising results you have not yet achieved. A cherry private isn't much different than a cherry businessperson. Nobody trusts the untested but eager cherry private. After an eager cherry private successfully completes a few training events, deployments, or patrols, he earns the trust of the team. Business works the same way; many of your best future opportunities come from trust built on value you patiently provided in the past, not from your cleverly worded promises.

Hurry up and provide value to your customers and team, but wait for the financial results. Develop goodwill quickly because it can take years to fully monetize. Not everybody needs your product or service immediately. While a few may need it now, most will want it later, and if you develop a strong reputation for value, they will keep coming back to you. You spend a lifetime building your reputation; don't make the mistake of cashing in goodwill too soon because of impatience.

WAITING TO STRIKE

One of the most important lessons of the hurry-up-and-wait principle is that there is never a perfect time for anything. That is exactly why the sooner you are ready, the more time you have, and thus the more opportunities. Your customers buy when they are ready, not when you are ready. So if your ideal customer is ready to buy and you're not ready to meet their needs, you just lost the sale. The same is true of your best future employees.

Most of your best employees five years from now don't work for you yet. Chances are good they will never be unemployed in the next five years. So how are you going to hire them? You are going to hurry up and wait. Start recruiting them immediately. Of course, they are not interested right now. They are happy with their current team, their position, their salary, and their opportunities for advancement.

However, in the next few years, they will have moments of uncertainty when they feel unhappy with their team, position, compensation, or future opportunities. Because you contacted them early and often with your recruiting pitch and they see your growth, your team, and your brand, they think the grass may be greener on your side of the fence. Too often, leaders wait until they need the specific skill set to recruit the right person. By failing to hurry up to let the person with the skills know you are interested in them years before you need them, you end up spending tens of thousands of dollars on a recruiter to fill the position and possibly hundreds of thousands of dollars in lost productivity because your company cannot function at its capacity until you find, hire, onboard, and train that person.

I recruited one of my leaders for four years before she joined our team. This highly experienced leader had positioned herself to become the director of her organization. During those four years, all signs pointed to her taking the reins and reaching the apex of her career. Guess what happened when she was unjustly passed over and her dream job was given to a less qualified candidate? She didn't call me! However, because I made it a point to check in with her every ninety days, when I met her for lunch, she launched into her disappointment and her concern about her next opportunity. I had waited years for this moment, and I readily offered her a key leadership role on my team at that lunch. She accepted two days later after we worked out the details.

Another leader with a completely different skill set had been a friend of mine for years. Based on his credentials and current role in a much larger organization, I didn't believe he would ever join my team. However, I made it clear to him that if he ever felt like he needed a challenge, our door was open, and we were saving a chair for him at the leadership table.

Over the years, he rose to the top of his organization's leadership team. He sat in the inner circle of a highly profitable tight-knit group of leaders with a stellar reputation for performance. Then, one day the CEO retired. A week later the COO resigned under less than favorable circumstances. An internal investigation led to the termination of several key leaders. The company took a beating publicly and financially. My friend weathered the storm and picked up the pieces. However, within a year, the replacement leaders chosen by the board had created a toxic environment of distrust and fear.

My friend had been preparing to jump ship for two months when I texted him, asking whether he knew anyone who might be able to fill a key role that was going to open up in our firm. At the time, I didn't think I had a chance of ever hiring him. After I sent him the details of the position, he responded, "I have a few names I will forward you, but I'd like to talk to you about whether you believe I'm qualified for the position." My response: "Don't send the names. Can we meet for lunch or dinner tomorrow?"

I sounded pretty desperate, right? Perhaps. However, I don't like to pretend like I'm not excited when I get the opportunity to bring next-level talent to my team. I suck at playing it cool for top talent. I want the person I hurried up and waited for—for years—to feel my excitement. Of course, we still had to vet him, do background checks, and follow our HR hiring process, but I had been waiting to hire him for so long that I knew everything I needed to know about him. Most importantly, I knew he was the right leader for the position.

The sooner you let them know you want them on your team, the better your odds of getting them.

AFTER-ACTION REVIEW

Sustain

1. Show up early and show up prepared. Hurry up and wait to build trust by being at the right place, at the right time, in the right uniform.

2. When you're ready, time is on your side. Don't force something just because you're ready.

3. Patience provides tactical advantages and builds credibility.

Improve

1. Greatness requires consistent compounding of excellent results. Start working on those results now.

2. Early success does not always mean you are ready to proceed to the next challenge.

3. Your prospects make decisions when they're ready, not when you're ready.

4. Bonus: Don't wait too long. Be intentional about when, but don't wait for perfection. There is never a perfect time to do anything, but some hours or days are more advantageous than others (e.g., the best time to launch a new product or service, the best time to call prospects, the best time to return calls, or the best time to ask for a sale).

5

FIELDCRAFT: MAKING DO WITH WHAT YOU HAVE

Improvise, adapt, overcome.

—**Gunny Highway,** *Heartbreak Ridge*

No matter how much gear the military issues, when you're in the field, you inevitably need something you don't have to get the job done. Sometimes the equipment the Central Issue Facility (CIF) provides you has to be used in unintended ways. In the military, we must be resourceful. We don't get everything we request, and requirements constantly change. Militaries have budgets, just like businesses, families, and so forth. Without fail, every deployment or field problem reminds us there will always be equipment that we will not be able to get our hands on when we need it.

In the field, we utilize what's available. Our platoon sergeant taught us how to improvise and use fieldcraft to make a lean-to out of our poncho to keep the rain off us in cases where we failed to add our shelter half (small tents) to our oversized packing list—it somehow always manages to rain when we're in the field. He taught us how to make a floating raft out of our rucksacks and wet-weather bags, and a flotation device with our trousers. He used 550 cord and 100 mph tape (also known as parachute cord and duct tape) to fix any equipment problem.

Resourcefulness is intrinsic to the military, and the fieldcraft lessons we learned from our platoon sergeant helped make life a little more tolerable. However, fieldcraft also saved lives and limbs with inventions such as the field-expedient splint made from sticks and the field dressing we all wear on our kit, and field-expedient litter to evacuate an immobile casualty using long tree branches and our issued ponchos.

In fact, some of the world's most important medical breakthroughs were born out of necessity during wartime. Soldiers first used tourniquets centuries ago during combat. An army doctor developed the first ambulance system during the Civil War. Penicillin was first mass-produced during World War II. The most impactful advances in anesthesia, sanitation, prosthetics, and plastic surgery have all come from combat innovation.

Breakthroughs in what we can create with our gear have taken place as well. If you've spent twenty years in the military, you have probably gone to CIF multiple times for reissues—going from the steel pot helmet to the Kevlar helmet to the Advanced Combat Helmet (ACH). You went through having a flak vest to metal plates to the porcelain plates of the Interceptor Multi-Threat Body Armor System (IBA) to better protect your torso from bullets. As the military field tests its equipment, it finds more effective solutions.

These breakthroughs will continue. New and innovative equipment eventually becomes obsolete, replaced by better gear. And if the new gear does not withstand the combat environment, it's only a matter of time before that gear becomes obsolete, replaced by a superior invention.

FIELDCRAFT IS ABOUT RESOURCEFULNESS

Problems attached with resourcefulness cause breakthroughs. When terrorists began to successfully attack Humvees with improvised explosive devices (IEDs), the army developed the Mine-Resistant Ambush Protected (MRAP) vehicle, built with a V shape in the middle to displace the detonation better and to better protect the soldiers in the vehicle. While the MRAP did not perfectly solve the problem, the breakthrough appeared to reduce the effectiveness of enemy IEDs and improved the survivability of convoy operations and mounted soldiers on patrol.

The MRAP had little to do with fieldcraft per se but came from the same innovative thinking. It was discontinued after a few years, proving that fieldcraft is often a temporary solution, and sometimes it only feels like a solution. It did address the political outcry that we were failing to protect our deployed soldiers who were getting blown up in Humvees every day, which had helped fund the project.

However, not all great projects get funded. Dream big, of course, and believe that the government (or, in the civilian sector, our company) will spend the money necessary to get us the best products and equipment to complete our jobs, but the truth of the matter is that budgets will always constrain what can be done. This is why veterans cringe when civilian truck companies brag about their "military grade" vehicles. We all know that military grade means the lowest bidder made it to the minimum specs. In other words, it's a piece of shit.

Military budgets swing back and forth with political sentiment. I served in the military long enough to see the pendulum of massive budget swing back and forth. When I deployed to Iraq, we seemed to get everything we requested; but six years earlier in Bosnia, the army wouldn't even up-armor our Humvees. At the unit level, we had no budget for CamelBak drinking systems, multitools, and high-power flashlights that we ended up purchasing ourselves. Every organization experiences the same swings from abundance to scarcity. Sometimes, budgets give wiggle room; other times, they remain airtight.

*Providing logistical support in western Iraq near the
Euphrates River and Khan al-Baghdadi*

Occasionally, the lack of necessary equipment has nothing to do with the budget, and everything to do with the fact that the product you need doesn't yet exist. In times of war, servicemembers have built what they need in the very moment by using the items they have on hand. Food, shelter, weapons, communications devices, and anything else can be made in a time of need. It's all about resourcefulness and about the desire to take care of your team and complete your mission.

CIVILIAN FIELDCRAFT

In business, it's all too easy to complain that budget restrictions are holding you back from completing your mission on time or to standard. The same goes for your personal life and your personal budgeting. It's too easy to claim that you would be successful if only you had all the right tools or the money necessary to buy those tools. With this logic, everyone would be successful if they just had all the resources. And yet we still see well-funded companies fail often. It seems they get used to having the cash to fund everything they need, but as soon as they face adversity and must scrounge for cash, they crumble.

True leaders know how to improvise, and they do it every day with not enough people, not enough resources, and not enough time. Leaders plan for restrictions and limitations and complete the mission to standard regardless of those obstacles. You need to know what you absolutely must accomplish, the minimum resources you need, all the resources at your disposal, and the resources you must acquire. Never be wasteful. Use your creative wisdom and intuition to prioritize and take actions to get results. If you don't have enough time and money to solve all the problems, suck it up and live with the low-priority problems that, if solved, would not move the needle.

If you have the raw materials, you can build nearly anything. I've seen people build spreadsheets on Microsoft Excel that outperform million-dollar software systems. I personally invested in software and technology programs that failed after months of lost effort and productivity and tens of thousands of dollars, only to find a simpler, less expensive solution. Generally, the higher the budget, the more room for error, but having the resources to succeed does not guarantee success. In fact, too many resources can bring a false sense of confidence. Every year, companies with millions of dollars of private-equity-invested funds fail.

Brendan Ballou's book *Plunder: Private Equity's Plan to Pillage America* reports that private equity firms are responsible for nearly six hundred thousand retail job losses.[1] It states that companies bought by private equity firms are ten times as likely to go bankrupt as those that aren't.[2] A 2015 Harvard study that revealed more than fifty companies had been forced into bankruptcy by private equity firms.[3] Twenty percent of private equity takeovers result in bankruptcy, ten times the rate for non-private-equity firms, according to a recent California Polytechnic State University study.[4]

What is wasteful? Do you need to buy a desk, or should you fieldcraft a desk out of old crates and a wooden door? Remember that fieldcraft isn't just about comfort; it's about efficiency. Throughout your career you will make and lose money, but you will never regain time you spent trying to save money. If the time you expend on fieldcraft does not make you more efficient, you may be stepping over dollars to pick up pennies.

When I arrived at Al Asad, Iraq, I arrived with the advanced party (ADVON). My first sergeant was traveling with the main body so that I could spend a few days in country before dealing with all the chaos of connexes (shipping containers) and property book issues that come with a transfer of authority. To my surprise, my counterpart picked me up at the airfield in a small Toyota pickup truck. The cheerful captain explained that inside the wire, troops traveled in gator vehicles and non-tactical vehicles (NTVs)—civilian trucks and SUVs—to save wear and tear on the up-armored Humvees. Plus, base rules required you to wear your helmet and IBA only in tactical vehicles, not in NTVs!

The goal of the NTV was to transport soldiers and marines on base more simply, quickly, and cheaply. During that time, up-armored Humvees, NTVs, and tracked vehicles all traveled on the same roads. Military police (MPs) scurried around the base warning drivers to slow down, or their name would be turned in to the base commander. We laughed at them, until they implemented field-expedient speed bumps by laying old tank tracks across the roads to slow on-base travel. At first, I just chalked this up to fieldcraft, but after a couple months of chewed-up tires from the tank tracks, I chalked it up to stupidity. Fieldcraft should make maximum use of military equipment, not destroy it.

Budgets might not allow you to provide your team with the most innovative software or the most efficient processes. As a veteran, you have the experience of being resourceful and can step up and be the leader your team needs in those times when they might be the most desperate.

In the military, like life, scarcity must be considered in your planning. If you run out of ammunition, water, or food, you will become combat ineffective. In business, if you run out of cash, your business will die. Scarcity is real even if you have an "abundance mindset." Fortunately, as a veteran, you know how to be scrappy and agile. In rapidly growing companies, the fight for resources can be fierce within the organization. You know that to achieve your goals, you must hire more team members, increase your marketing spend, purchase new technology tools, expand your physical footprint, and so forth. Eventually you face the reality that the main effort will get the necessary resources, and the other efforts must "find a way" to make it work.

Of course, the marketing team will complain they need more budget spend to feed qualified leads to the sales team. The sales team will claim they need better software and more salespeople. The IT team will request equipment upgrades, external cyber-security audits, and more engineers. The operations team will demand more of everything. The finance team may be the only team not requesting anything but begging you to stay within the budget.

Despite what gurus claim on social media, you cannot grow into a highly effective and efficient company overnight. First, you can't afford it. Second, even if you could afford it, you may not have the necessary experience to make it happen. Fieldcraft, after all, is really just solving a problem with inadequate immediate resources and reconfiguring and testing those resources until it works.

GUERILLA FIELDCRAFT

While large armies relatively equal in might may fight using conventional linear wars, outnumbered, outgunned, "inferior" forces often resort to guerilla warfare, an asymmetric fighting strategy to minimize their opponent's tactical advantage and level the playing field. To borrow the phrase of Patrick M. Malone's book of the same name, small-banded opportunists prefer "the skulking way of war."[5]

Smaller, innovative companies use marketing fieldcraft to maximize their marketing efforts in competitive landscapes. If you don't have the capital to adequately market your product against your competitors, you must maximize your resources and opportunities with unconventional tactics. Guerilla marketing utilizes the same principles as guerrilla warfare. If you can't go toe to toe and pound for pound against your competitor, you resort to unconventional warfare. You only engage where you can win, and you don't waste resources fighting where you cannot.

Some of today's biggest brands successfully used guerilla marketing to make giant leaps when they lacked the resources to go head-to-head with more powerful competitors in their markets. For example, in front of the building hosting PayPal's 2010 developer conference, competitor WePay placed a giant block of ice with hundreds of dollars frozen beneath the surface and note reading: "PayPal freezes your accounts!"

The growth of Salesforce is attributed to aggressive guerrilla marketing tactics pulled off by CEO Marc Benioff. In one instance, Benioff hired fake protesters to disrupt the leading competitor's conference. Another time he rented all the taxis at a rival's French event to give attendees a forty-five-minute pitch while driving them to the event in another.

Guerilla marketing does not have to be as wild or aggressive for it to create a solid return on investment. Some successful marketing campaigns include handing out fliers in key areas of likely customers, wearing chicken suits while holding a sign, or sending promotional newsletters to a hypertargeted audience of ideal customers.

Business is filled with opportunities to collaborate with other like-minded allies. We've collaborated with other brands, partnered with communities and other industries, and cohosted events. In many ways, the smaller, more personal marketing efforts yielded a much greater return on investment over the years. Having a strong connection with a few consumers who resonate with your brand can be much more effective than blasting your message to millions of people who don't know anything about your company and don't need your product or service. The return on relationships is always greater than the return on messaging.

Remember that every business faces the same problems, and we can often work together to solve them. Years ago, we leased a space that we wanted to grow into. Even though our revenue didn't reflect it, we had run out of physical space. We had nine employees working out of four offices, and we had another employee working out of what can only be described as a broom closet. When the building next door became available, we jumped at the opportunity to acquire it. We only needed half the space, so we separated the building into two separate suites. We rented the second suite out to a veteran-owned karate studio that operated after business hours. The lease helped us pay the rent for another eighteen months until our growing head count required us to take over the karate studio and make offices out of it.

What the military taught you about fieldcraft can be used everywhere. In lean times and in austere conditions you must learn to make the most of what you have. In the military, like in business, you will experience times when you just don't have the resources to get what you need. In those moments, you will have to figure it out and fieldcraft a solution with the equipment or cash you have available. When someone says it's impossible to complete a mission with limited resources, that just means they can't figure it out. If someone else lacks the ingenuity and creativity to get the mission done, it doesn't mean you can't do it. Lack of resources is always a reason for failure, but it's not always a valid excuse.

AFTER-ACTION REVIEW

Sustain

1. Scarcity is real. Deal with it.

2. While there is no shortage of success, you must constantly overcome shortages of money and time.

3. Fieldcraft is about survival. If you can't afford the solution, you must find a way.

Improve

1. If you are not the eight-hundred-pound gorilla in your market, consider using guerrilla tactics to drive business.

2. Leaders innovate. Stop whining about not having enough resources.

3. Not all your efforts will be adequately funded all the time. Prioritize the main effort and use fieldcraft when necessary.

6

PRIORITIES OF WORK

People who can focus, get things done.
People who can prioritize, get the right things done.

—John Maeda, X post

Priorities of work tell us the things we need to do, regardless of how hard or unpopular they are with our teams.

I remember one of my first training exercises. We started before dawn, conducted three platoon lanes (missions), and then started marching toward the next training area. We had been humping fifty-pound rucksacks for hours (the trainers had weighed our rucksacks to ensure we got the maximum training value), and when we halted and took a knee, it was dark. We proceeded to fumble our way through the uneven terrain setting up a triangle-shaped patrol base.

At the end of a long day of patrolling, we all just wanted to do the rucksack flop, eat chow, change socks, warm up, and go to sleep. No one wanted to do weapons maintenance, and certainly no one wanted to dig or improve fighting positions. This, however, is where we began the priorities of work: a series of activities completed sequentially. Occupy patrol base, set up security, emplace crew-served weapons, conduct sector sketches, perform weapons maintenance, eat, take care of personal hygiene, and never stop pulling security while you fortify your position. We worked through the list of priorities in order, completing one before starting the next.

Too often, we allow what is comfortable to supplant what is the more difficult right. Just as the lives of your team members may depend on your willingness to adhere to these principles in combat, your business survival may depend on your ability to prioritize and execute difficult, unpopular tasks.

Just like the patrol base, priorities of work and the discipline to follow them remain key ingredients in productivity in any endeavor. In 1918, Charles Schwab, who owned Bethlehem Steel, the second-largest steel company in the United States, hired Ivy Lee as a consultant to help him increase steel production. Schwab told Lee that his team knew what they needed to do, but they were failing to do it. Lee told Schwab that he needed to spend fifteen minutes with each executive on Schwab's team, and then, ninety days following the advice to the executives, Schwab was to send Lee a check for the value of his guidance.

Lee's advice to Schwab's executives was this: Every day, write down the top six things you need to do in order of importance. Start working on number one on your list, and do not move on to number two until you've completed number one. Complete each task in order of importance from your list without distraction before moving to the next task. After ninety days, Schwab sent Lee a check for $25,000, which is equivalent to almost $500,000 today. Setting priorities and following them in order of importance was the only advice Schwab's executives needed.[1]

I follow the same advice but limit my daily priorities to three or five at most. At the end of each day, I create a list of the top things I need to do the following day. The next morning, I do the first thing on the list until it's done before moving to number two. I complete number two before moving on to number three, and so on. I budget time on my calendar for each task, so it looks like Table 1.

While completing the priority task, I do not check email, social media, text messages, or take phone calls. Productivity requires prioritization. When I start checking emails, I am

Table 1. My daily list of priorities

MAY 27, 2023		
PRIORITY 1	0800–1000	Draft outline of next year's business plan
PRIORITY 2	1030–1130	Weekly key leader meeting
PRIORITY 3	1300–1400	Meet with website team to discuss vision implementation
PRIORITY 4	1430–1515	Review proposed marketing materials for approval
PRIORITY 5	1600–1630	Write thank-you notes

letting someone else set my priorities. If my email inbox dictates my next action, I'm no longer taking initiative, I'm reacting to someone else's priorities. You are the commander of your life and the commander of your business. You set the priorities for your team and for yourself.

Of course, this looks easier than it will be to execute. You want that dopamine hit from the next message. Fortunately, the military taught you discipline. Complete the first task on your list; then go to email or respond as necessary during your breaks. Email is routine correspondence. You don't need to respond immediately (even if the sender marked it urgent). Ultimately, checking your email once a day or ten times a day doesn't matter. What matters is that you mark on your calendar when you will check it and you stick to that schedule; you control incoming communications, and those communications don't run your business. While you probably work much longer hours than eight to five most days, you don't need to plan to work longer hours every day. Table 2 is an example of how setting priorities may look in your calendar.

But what about emergencies and potential customers who I need to service immediately? Don't those take precedence over my priorities? Yes, if you let them. When I interviewed my first COO, I took him through a reality-based leadership exercise to better understand how he would interact with team members during times of potential high conflict. After I delivered the fact pattern to him, he said, "As a leader, whenever possible, put a person between yourself and the problem." What he meant was to create some space.

Table 2. Priority list example

MAY 27, 2023		
PRIORITY 1	0800-1000	Complete outline of next year's business plan
	1000-1030	Check and respond to emails, texts, and social media messages; break
PRIORITY 2	1030-1130	Weekly key leader meeting
	1130-1300	Lunch with referral source and check in with second in command
PRIORITY 3	1300-1400	Meet with website team to discuss vision implementation
	1400-1430	Check and respond to emails, texts; break
PRIORITY 4	1430-1515	Review proposed marketing materials for approval
	1515-1600	Buffer time for any emergencies, review weekly, monthly priorities
PRIORITY 5	1600-1630	Write thank-you notes
	1630-1645	Complete tomorrow's priority list
	1645-1700	Review daily metrics

As leaders, we want to rush in, lead by example, and solve the problem to show the team how to quickly and efficiently handle emergencies. We do this because we do not want a problem to linger and be ignored, or worse, grow into a bigger problem. But if we respond to emergencies all day, we never reach our priorities.

Task a subordinate leader with taking point on emergencies. Not only will you have a person between you and the problem if the emergency affects your schedule, but you also have empowered a leader who may resolve the emergency without your awareness of it. You just saved time and stress resolving an emergency that didn't require your involvement.

But how will my team know which emergencies to resolve without me? You will tell them. In the military, every commander published commander's critical information requirements (CCIR). If any "emergency" qualified as CCIR, you would wake up the boss in the middle of the night to give him situational awareness and let him decide whether he would personally get involved. The military has now differentiated CCIR from "wake up" requirements, finding that prearranged decision requirements may be too narrow to be effective. However, you employ leaders in your organization for this very reason. If something falls outside of your "do not disturb" criteria, the leaders should be smart enough to "wake you up" if they deem your involvement necessary.

A few years ago, at a quarterly meeting, several team members praised and recognized our chief technology officer (CTO) for responding to a late-Friday-night network outage and having the network up and running by 0600 Saturday morning. Prior to the meeting, I had no idea the network had gone down; nor did I know our CTO had worked through the night to fix it. While I would have liked to know about the network problem and the heroic efforts and commitment of our CTO, there was nothing I could have done to improve the outcome. The CTO, taking the initiative to solve the problem without alerting me demonstrated that my involvement in the emergency wasn't absolutely unnecessary.

The other objection I hear to creating a priority calendar is: but shouldn't I have "white space" on my calendar to pursue unplanned opportunities? You do. Not only do you have scheduled breaks, but every time hack in between the priorities is "white space." If it's not one of your listed priorities, you can be flexible. The only rigidity in your schedule is the time you protect for your priorities. You design your calendar to focus on priorities, but you still have large chunks of nonpriority time to complete routine tasks that you are not yet able to delegate.

But what if I don't complete priority 1 in the allotted two-hour time frame? Then you continue working into the priority 2 time allotment. At the end of the day, you may only make it through your first two priorities. If this happens, priorities 3 to 5 get moved to the following day. This way, when you assess your top five priorities for the next day, you already have three from the previous day.

But I committed to the five priorities today; don't I need to get them all done today? Ideally, yes, but often we underestimate the amount of time it takes to complete a project, because we underestimate the time it takes to complete all the action steps. I frequently fail to account for all the action steps required to complete a project I have never previously attempted. Some priority projects that I scheduled for two hours on my calendar take me two days to complete. That's right, two days on one priority. This meant I had to delay or kill other priorities.

Some priorities turn out to not be priorities. If that is the case, just kill the task. As Arianna Huffington said, "You can complete a project by dropping it."[2]

REMOVE YOURSELF FROM THE FOXHOLE TO GET THE BEST VIEW

There is a reason why the platoon leader positions himself at the center of the patrol base and not in a fighting position on the perimeter. The leader must see the battlespace and understand the common operating picture (COP) to visualize the current battlefield as well as the battlefield of the near future. Thus, while the patrol base functions on systematized priorities of work, which are almost always the same, the platoon leader must think beyond current activities to focus on the next priorities.

To survive, the team must understand the systematized priorities. As a leader, you establish and publish priorities for your team. In the army, the noncommissioned officers handle the day to day, which allows the officers to plan for the future. The officer empowers the noncommissioned officers to deviate from assigned priorities of work when necessary because the noncommissioned officers understand their leaders' intent. Often, leaders set too many priorities, resulting in a burned-out team. Leaders fear that if they do not prioritize enough missions, they will not execute rapidly enough. But, as the saying goes, "If everything is a priority, nothing is a priority." So how does a leader set priorities?

DO WHAT MOVES THE NEEDLE THE MOST

Vietnam veteran and fighter pilot Jeff Sutherland learned how to prioritize and control risk in air force training in a four-step model designed by Colonel John Boyd called the OODA loop: observe, orient, decide, and act. In his book *Scrum: The Art of Doing Twice the Work in Half the Time*, Sutherland explains that while hesitation got pilots killed, so did foolhardiness.[3] You need a decision framework to ensure you make the best decisions quickly. As you set priorities, you observe, orient, decide, act, and then start over in a loop. It's not that you just decide to do the thing that will create the biggest impact, it is that you follow the steps to determine (1) what will move the needle the most and (2) how you will do it based on your current operating environment.

Airbnb began with a couple of roommates needing to earn rent money; they converted their apartment into a makeshift bed and breakfast and offered it to attendees of a conference in San Francisco because there was a shortage of accommodations. After successfully hosting three people on air mattresses, they knew they had something special, and, in 2008, they tried to launch what they called Air Bed and Breakfast for the SXSW Conference and the Democratic National Convention. When both failed, they designed and sold presidential-themed breakfast cereals, focusing on the "breakfast" part of their brand. This moved the needle enough to help them pay off some debt they'd been accumulating and gain some media coverage, but they still needed a jumping-off point to start growing. They got a big opportunity, thanks to their persistence, in the form of a little seed funding and some great mentoring from Paul Graham, founder of Y Combinator. He suggested they focus on New York, the hottest subset of the market, put a lot of energy into supporting the hosts to create great experiences, and help them with ratings and photos. Once they set these new priorities, the needle began to move a lot.

FIND OUT WHAT IS MOST IMPORTANT, AND THEN DO THAT FIRST

Too often, small companies concern themselves with defensive priorities rather than going on the offense. In the military, you only stay in a defense posture long enough to prepare to go back on offense. The patrol base, while defensive in nature, is merely the launching pad for future offensive operations. Cash-generating activities should always be a priority. If your core business is generating enough cash for you to invest in other products or services, great. Maybe it's time to go on the offensive. The problem comes when you've spent too much time, focus, and money on the latest venture, and your core business is stalling out and not producing the funds needed to sustain the new line of business.

Several times at Berry Law we launched new services, new technology platforms, and new initiatives that failed. We understood the risk and the potential upside, and we invested accordingly. We ensured the core business remained the priority for our budgets and focus. We also predefined success for our new ventures by listing what must be true by a specific date on the calendar for the project to be a success. If we hit all the criteria, the project was a go, and we would continue to invest. If we did not hit every criterion, it was a no-go, and we ceased the project. We ruthlessly prioritized future offensive operations because we knew we would never be able to pursue every great opportunity.

Many leaders fail to adequately prioritize because they confuse priority with the "speed" at which they implement. High-priority initiatives may take several months or years to complete. Implementing a new sales or financial management system often takes months to implement even though the vendor promises it will take only thirty days. Sometimes the vendor salesperson is simply not in sync with the engineers on their own team or does not fully understand the complexity of your organization. Other times, your organization will need to implement an unexpectedly long change-management process to ensure you can sustain operations during all phases of a major project.

As you experience periods of rapid growth, you will have to pivot priorities from growth to risk mitigation. Some of our highest-priority IT projects every year focus on enhancing our cybersecurity, at the cost of pursuing the latest tech systems. While investing in cybersecurity does little for our immediate growth, we prioritize it because it mitigates risk and helps us avoid catastrophic problems. We also set priorities that protect us from legal, financial, or reputational risk the same way.

So where do you focus your priorities, understanding that not every priority will supercharge the growth of your team?

Focus on your biggest opportunities and your biggest threats. Of course, you will be wrong from time to time, and when you are, acknowledge it, pivot, and reset your priorities.

AFTER-ACTION REVIEW

Sustain

1. Establish security. Protect your cash flow.

2. Focus efforts on the biggest opportunities and relationships.

3. Do the basic blocking and tackling well, before adding complexity.

Improve

1. If the action you're contemplating doesn't move the needle in the direction of progress, don't do it unless it's necessary.

2. If it's not necessary or you can't measure the impact of your efforts, stop doing it.

3. When everything is a priority, nothing is a priority.

7

CONDUCT RISK ASSESSMENTS

An ounce of prevention is worth a pound of cure.

—Benjamin Franklin, "On Protection of Towns from Fire"

L eaders take risks. It's the reason others follow.

On my first day at Fort Benning, July 5, 1997, my dad and I sat at the officer's club bar for dinner.

"My son just received his commission," my dad said to the Special Forces colonel. "If you have advice for him here, what would it be?"

What that Special Forces colonel said has stuck with me ever since: "Leaders take sensible risks; they don't take stupid risks." I thought back to that advice during my days at Fort Benning, and at many points thereafter. As it turned out, they were some of the truest words I would hear in my time in the military.

The colonel correctly stated that leaders *must* take risks. There is risk in action. If we attack, there is a risk of suffering casualties. At the same time, there is risk in *inaction*. By doing nothing, we allow the enemy to attack us and run the risk of suffering yet *more* casualties.

As leaders we must maximize opportunities to use systems that mitigate risk. In the army, specifically, we used a risk assessment known as the DRAW, or the Deliberate Risk Assessment Worksheet. This worksheet identifies hazards and risks and improves our awareness of operating environments. It helps leaders eliminate unnecessary risks while mitigating the necessary ones. The DRAW and other preliminary assessments explore implications but never eliminate all negative consequences. We plan for risk, we plan to mitigate risk, and we ultimately decide, after we calculate the reduced risk, whether we still want to take the action.

THE CALCULATED RISK

Every veteran has been exposed to the risks of a live-fire range. Consider unmitigated risk associated with a platoon of soldiers firing live ammunition. The initial risk assignment is catastrophic, because one of the identified risks is that someone could get shot in the face and die. Working through the risk matrix, we assign range safety personnel, on-site familiarization training, a control tower with visibility of every firing position and shooter, and procedures for ammo distribution, handling, and recoupment. Through these mitigating factors, we reduce the risk to an acceptable level. The goal of risk management in business operations, like military training, is not to abandon all risky behavior; rather, it's to mitigate risk to an acceptable level. Results occur in the case of both action and inaction. Doing something will get a result, and doing nothing will also get a result. The key is to make the risk decision based on the action or inaction most likely to achieve desired results. Leaders need to focus on accomplishing the mission at hand but also must know that we cannot wastefully expend human capital in the process. We must be clear on our objectives and only take the risks necessary to achieve them.

At the same time, we must understand that without taking serious risks, our objectives will never be achieved. In our personal world, within our family, our business, or our career, we must take risks if we want to reap the rewards. If nobody ever took risks, we would not have the products or processes we have today, which have led us to live such extraordinary lives.

Every great result requires risk, but recklessness is unacceptable. I want to caution you with a story I heard about Warren Buffett, pulled from a book called *The Road Less Stupid* by Keith J. Cunningham. Buffett was golfing with a group of friends. At a par three hole, a friend said, "Warren, I'll bet $20 you don't hit a hole-in-one." Warren asked what odds he would get. The friend offered one thousand-to-one odds, meaning if Buffett made the hole-in-one, he would get $20,000, but if he missed, he would only have to pay $20. Without hesitation Buffett rejected the bet, knowing the odds of hitting a hole-in-one were about as close to zero as they could be. Surprised, the fellow golfer asked Buffett, "What's twenty dollars to you?"

The billionaire responded, "Stupid in small things, stupid in big things."[1]

Remember the quote commonly attributed to General Patton, "You fight like you train"? Same concept.

As leaders, we must always weigh the odds. We must always weigh the risk. We all run into "opportunities" where we assess the risk as low and the possible reward as high, but we must never squander our team's focus on the "opportunity" to make a quick buck. There are plenty of ways to make a little bit more money by offering a new product or service with seemingly little effort or risk. When I find myself facing a low-risk, low-effort, low-reward opportunity, I usually pass. I pass because it is not worth the loss of focus on our main effort.

There are countless examples of businesses taking a big risk and failing. In 1985, for instance, Coca-Cola debuted a new formula marketed as New Coke, which they thought would be more popular than its chief rival, Pepsi. Coke famously locked away its original formula in a bank vault. The response was so overwhelmingly negative that Coke went back to its original formula within a few weeks, having underestimated the consumer's loyal connection to the brand. Keurig, one of the most popular single-serve coffee maker brands, used in just under forty million households as of 2024, debuted the Keurig Kold in October of 2015. The machine offered consumers a way to make their own soft drinks, like Coca-Cola, among other cold beverages, at home. In less than a year, the company pulled the product from the shelves and offered full refunds to consumers. Cost, convenience, and consumer trends toward healthier alternatives provided by brands such as SodaStream all led to Keurig Kold's massive flop. The risk did not pay off, but the

Keurig brand survived and shifted its focus back to coffee makers. With brand recognition topping at 90 percent, it boasted nine straight years of market share gains as of 2023.[2]

One lesson from these major flops is that big corporations budget for risk. They know failure is necessary for success. They rarely engage in a "bet the company" or "burn the ships" strategy. They develop contingency plans, and they make sure they can survive even if the venture fails.

For smaller businesses, one of the toughest lessons is that not all business is good business. I've witnessed firsthand the blind risks leaders take when they lack the discipline to stick to their core focus. They take on a client outside the scope of their core services to make a bit more money. This one-off decision, at best, causes them to lose money, and at worst, puts them in deep trouble.

I see this all the time in less experienced lawyers. A case comes into the office; the legal problem is outside the scope of the practice areas the lawyer regularly handles. The client convinces the lawyer the case is worth millions and wants the lawyer to take the case on a contingency basis, fronting all costs and expenses. The lawyer thinks it's a slam dunk case, based on what the client tells him and his own ignorance of this practice area.

Months later, the lawyer has invested hundreds of hours into the case, realizes he is in over his head, and is now spending sleepless nights trying to figure out how to get out of the case without damage to his reputation and professional credentials. What's worse, he's also caught in a sunk cost fallacy in which he thinks he's invested too much time to withdraw from the case even though he's facing hundreds of additional hours of fruitless work. Not only will he not get paid for his work, but he has pulled in other team members from the core business onto the case, and when he loses, they won't get paid either. They will have squandered time they could have put into the core business, which would have generated substantial revenue. Worst of all, the lawyer failed his client by not having the guts to refer the case to a more experienced lawyer in a better position to assess the merits of the case.

When you know what you're really seeking, you know what to avoid.

THE RISK OF FAILURE AND LEADERSHIP

Leaders know that inexperience increases the risk of failure. In the military, leaders constantly seek out their most experienced leaders for high-risk missions. Despite what eager, inexperienced subordinates claim, if you've never done it, you don't know how to do it. However, that does not mean inexperience makes risk unacceptable. At some point, we all must learn by doing. The leader's role is to keep the cost of learning and the associated risks low. Of course, experience does not eliminate the risk of failure either. Even our most experienced leaders fail from time to time. The key is to overcome the failure, learn from it, and not let it happen again. As leaders, our team will always forgive us when we own those failures and explain that, while we did not get the result we wanted, we made progress.

To mitigate risk, we must always do what is in the best interest of our team, our customers, and our future. When we inevitably fail, we notice the failure, analyze the risk so that we can address the problem head-on in a timely manner, and learn the lesson so it doesn't occur again. When we make the wrong decision, we face negative consequences, but the team will not lose faith in a good leader if we acknowledge the risk in an honest and straightforward manner. A good leader will not let a negative result stop all progress but will rather use the negative event to learn how to mitigate risk in the future.

In the military, everyone is a leader. When it comes to mitigating risk, we naturally follow the superior leader. We have all served in a unit where the top squad leader, rather than the platoon sergeant, *actually* runs the platoon, because the squad leader either has more combat experience or superior leadership skills. Team members will not follow an inferior leader for long. Teams follow the superior leader in the group regardless of title and rank. One key reason is safety; the more experienced or superior leader generally makes the team feel safer.

Leadership authority does not equate to leadership capability. The second lieutenant straight out of college with zero real-world leadership experience can become the leader of a platoon composed of several NCOs who have decades of combined leadership experience. The same can happen in the civilian sector, where a fool with a master's degree can join the company's leadership team despite lacking industry experience and practical leadership experience. Experience does not trump all, however: the true leader consistently performs at or above the standards regardless of her experience. A true leader personifies professionalism, and professionalism mitigates risk.

Rank and titles guarantee authority, not leadership. As a leader, you will need to take risks to provide your team with opportunities. You will need to weigh options. But most importantly, you will need to protect those who look up to you and who serve alongside you so they will fully commit to taking the risk with you.

CHEAP LESSONS

Learn from the mistakes of others. Remember back in boot camp or basic training where one recruit would screw up and the entire formation of thirty-six soldiers would be doing push-ups and flutter kicks for the next thirty minutes? In the military training environment, the hyperscrutiny makes it feel like someone is always screwing something up. That's how it works in business. Someone on the team screws up and the company pays for it, literally. As the leader, you face problems every day, and your job is to solve them. The endless cycle of problem/solution, problem/solution, problem/solution never ceases, so embrace it. Without problems we would not need leaders.

But what if you could learn from mistakes without having to pay for them? You can. Find an experienced mentor or join business leader peer groups such as Bunker Labs, Entrepreneurs' Organization, Young Presidents' Organization, Vistage, or better yet, peer groups in your industry. Most of these groups operate in confidentiality so you can learn from the mistakes of your peers. Not only can you learn from your peers, but you can vet ideas through them to see if anyone else has attempted what you plan to do and can tell you the mistakes to avoid.

Another way to learn from mistakes without having to pay too much for them, is to catch them early. Encourage your team to "go ugly early." If they sense a problem, they should report it through the chain of command. No problem gets better with time, and the sooner you as the leader learn about the problem, the sooner you can either fix it or take action to mitigate the risk of it getting worse. Often the damage caused by a delay or cover-up is far worse than the initial mistake that caused the problem. The longer the problem goes unaddressed, the greater the risk that it will become an expensive lesson. An infection treated early requires little effort and usually causes little harm. An untreated infection for a prolonged period may lead to amputation or death.

A DIME DROPPED IS A DIME WELL SPENT

"A dime dropped is a dime well spent." I heard a brigadier general say these words at the National Training Center decades ago. We had just completed our two-week training in "the box," and the general participated in our brigade AAR.

In the army, after every mission or training event, we conduct an AAR to learn what to sustain (keep doing) and what to improve (stop doing). Soldiers are notoriously tight-lipped at AARs because they don't want to call out their superiors and peers for mistakes or bad decisions. No soldier wants to look like a tattletale, a rat, suck-up, or a Monday-morning quarterback. Calling out the mistakes of team members makes you appear disloyal, arrogant, or mean-spirited. But the general went on to make it clear that the AAR is a zero attribution and zero retribution environment where we must be brutally honest to help our team improve. He said, "The risk of calling out a team member and hurting their ego is much more acceptable than the risk of keeping your mouth shut and letting that leader make the same mistake in combat."

Cheap lessons are learned in training, but only when we are honest enough to openly share them with the team. If you take the criticism personally, you're too soft to be a leader. In leadership, the most expensive lessons are those that cost us our credibility. As a leader, you make mistakes, and you learn from those mistakes—that is how you build character. While we can survive most mistakes, willful misconduct will cause permanent damage in the hearts and minds of your subordinates. Once you lose the trust of a subordinate, you will not likely regain it. Do not take risks that will cost you your credibility.

DANGEROUS TEAM MEMBERS

Similarly, do not tolerate team members who take risks with their credibility. While mistakes of skill are acceptable, mistakes of will are not. As a leader, if you allow misconduct, you condone it. The standard you allow is the standard you set. I'm not talking about daredevils and those fearless team members who seem to prefer challenging and difficult operations. I'm talking about the employees who operate mostly in gray areas of morals, ethics, or laws. They are easy to spot because they justify everything they do. When they make a mistake, they never make excuses, because they are always right. In fact, dangerous team members never even make room for the possibility of a mistake. They operate as if they earned some special privilege that allows them to act with impunity. They disregard company policies, always have a better way of doing things, and blatantly disrespect coworkers. Dangerous team members will take risks that could destroy your company.

INSURANCE FOR EVERYTHING

It's not only the dangerous team members who could ruin your business. Incompetent team members, inexperienced team members, and even *you* may make a bad decision that could put the company at risk. Fortunately, you can mitigate risk by carrying appropriate insurance. For most of us, insurance is an afterthought, a necessary evil, and something we want to pay as little as possible for. We see insurance as a penalty rather than an investment. However, insurance can be your best investment in mitigating risk, even though it may seem to be an investment in survival rather than growth. Inadequate insurance could be catastrophic to your business. As a leader, you must face the reality that you or a team member will occasionally take action or fail to take an action that puts the company at risk.

DELIBERATE DEFENSE

Insurance is not the only defensive practice to mitigate risk. Sometimes you must take a deliberate defensive position to advance. Just like in military operations, you may outrun your logistical tail. As tanks and Bradley Fighting Vehicles advance on the battlefield, the assets that fuel and maintain those vehicles must keep up. Without sufficient fuel and maintenance, your army cannot advance. When this happens, commanders set up a deliberate defense for a period long enough to rearm and refuel before going back on the offense.

In business, you cannot continually advance at top speed. From time to time, you will need to deliberately defend your gains before making another major offensive push. Sometimes the deliberate defensive position is dictated by changing economic conditions, and other times your rapid growth creates a vacuum in the organization where you need to retrain your team, hire for and onboard next-level talent, restructure your team, or make significant changes to your product or service to better serve the changing needs of your customer base.

YouTube started out as a dating site intended for people to make introductory videos. The technology was great and easy to use, but the site wasn't getting any users, so the founders decided to let go of the dating idea and just allowed it to be a site for people to upload any videos. The pivot paid off, and Google bought YouTube for $1.6 billion (about $5 per person in the United States) in 2006.

Slack was born out of a failing video game and an inspired pivot. Developer Stewart Butterfield had previously turned his first attempt at a video game into Flickr, which Yahoo! bought for $35 million. On his second attempt to create a video game, Butterfield had hefty venture capital investments of $17 million, and even though that afforded him the best software developers, after going through $10 million, he realized the game was too niche and was likely not going to succeed. As with his previous endeavor, he did not fall into the sunk cost fallacy; he realized the communication software the team had built to coordinate the project internally was better than anything on the market. He pivoted once again and turned the failing venture into the massively successful communication platform Slack.

TACTICAL PAUSE

Take a knee and drink water. The same maniacal focus that builds momentum and gets you traction can destroy you if you let it. When I was a battalion commander of a training school, I would often see officer candidates in leadership positions push themselves for days with little sleep. I would see NCOs push themselves past the point of exhaustion ensuring their soldiers were taken care of. We are human, and we must pause from time to time to regain our strength. If we don't, we will fail not only physically but mentally.

One of the key lessons I learned in Ranger School was that even the best leaders, when deprived of food and sleep, become ineffective. While several scientific studies demonstrate how severe physical stress hinders decision-making ability, I saw it happen firsthand. Some of my peers whom I greatly admired failed patrols, made bad decisions, lost the confidence of their teams, and even committed integrity violations when their bodies reached their breaking point. While I appreciated these leaders' grit and inability to accept defeat, their lack of self-awareness and judgment during periods of extreme fatigue shocked me.

Even the best leaders fail if they do not take care of themselves. Not only should you as the leader remind your subordinates to take a knee and drink water from time to time; you should also follow that advice. Remember that you are the multimillion-dollar tactical athlete. Eat like an athlete, sleep like an athlete, train like an athlete, and perform like an athlete. You should perform at your best every day just as we expect our athletes to be at their best every time they step on the field.

If you played sports in high school or college, you probably know the game day rituals. Team dinner the night before, an early light's out for a good night's sleep, team breakfast, walk-throughs, getting checked out by the team trainer, an inspection by the equipment manager, and then an hour of relaxation and visualization before the coach starts getting everybody fired up to get on the field. While many veterans have injuries that prevent us from performing like top athletes, that's no excuse to fail to optimize our minds and bodies for top performance.

As leaders, we often err on the side of rushing headlong into the fray. We misconceive tactical pauses as hesitation, indecisiveness, or weakness. Our training tells us to take the initiative, maintain the momentum throughout the battle, and never let up on the enemy. While we must maintain our aggressive nature, we must not ignore the common army-ism "There's generally a very fine line between hard core and stupid." A tactical pause will give you time to reflect on whether your future plans are hard core or just plain stupid.

THE VALUE OF RISK

Sometimes the greatest value in taking risks is gaining experience. Not only do we learn intensely through new experiences, but we develop leaders when we take a risk and bet on them. Every task you delegate to a subordinate leader assumes a risk. If the subordinate successfully completes the mission, you delegated appropriately. If the subordinate fails the mission, you abdicated your responsibility as a leader. This is the great paradox of leadership. You are responsible for everything, but you must also develop leaders by providing them the opportunity to handle the most challenging tasks your organization faces.

If you take a big risk, you may lose money, influence, friends, or even your company. But you will never lose the experience you gained in taking the risk. If you currently hold a leadership position in a private company, ask yourself this question: If I lost everything tomorrow, how long would it take me to rebuild? I know this sounds like the famous Lee Greenwood song, but if all the things you worked for all your life were gone, could you do it again? If you're a leader, the answer is yes. Most investors want to work with entrepreneurs who have tasted the experience of failure.

Embrace risk. Mitigate it, reduce it, take out insurance against it, and then recalculate it. Fortune favors the bold, not the stupid.

As a leader, you delegate authority, but not responsibility. You don't relieve yourself of culpability for outcomes by virtue of delegation.

AFTER-ACTION REVIEW

Sustain

1. Leaders take calculated risks.

2. Mitigate risks through planning.

3. Budget for risks.

Improve

1. Make contingency plans—burn the ships sparingly.

2. Buy insurance—you now have something to lose.

3. Even if you lose everything, you never lose an experience.

Part II

THRIVE

8

RIDE THE LIGHTNING— THE RUNAWAY GUN

In improvisation, there are no mistakes.

—Attributed to Miles Davis

One of the first lessons you learn in the military is to expect every day to be an uphill climb. Every single day challenges us to get better by doing the hard work that most people can't and won't do. Some days it seems we lose ground despite our best efforts. Then, out of nowhere, we get blasted with momentum that we could not have foreseen. It's as if, after days of trudging through slow terrain in a swamp, on foot, you find yourself on the highway going a hundred miles an hour in a comfortable sports car with the air-conditioning blasting. You don't know whether to enjoy it or to fear it, but you do know it won't last. So which is the better course of action, to slow down or step on the gas? The machine gunner faces the same quandary when experiencing a "runaway gun."

If you've ever fired an M60, the M240B, or even the Saw (M249), you know machine guns will malfunction from time to time. With your traditional M4 or M16 rifle, when the weapon jams and ceases to fire, it's an easy problem to solve: you just need to clear the breach, chamber another round, and squeeze the trigger. Yet with larger, belt-fed weapons that fire several rounds per trigger squeeze, the problem isn't always that easy. Belt-fed machine guns can continue to fire even after your finger has left the trigger.

These are the moments when you will need to decide whether to break the belt of ammunition or "ride the lightning." In a high-stress situation, as rounds dispense from the barrel at a pace of hundreds of bullets per minute, you continue aiming the weapon downrange while deciding whether you want to break the belt to end the problem quickly or ride the lightning and let that weapon fire until all the ammo on the belt has run through.

Your platoon sergeant will tell you to ride the lightning. He or she will tell you that you need to be decisive in the moment, even as your adrenaline is at an all-time high and the momentum of the weapon is dictating the pace. Despite all of this, you still need to remain calm and focused.

As the belt continues to feed itself into a malfunctioning weapon that fires of its own accord, you focus on the targets downrange. If you panic, you could kill someone outside the range fan. But if you stay focused and keep the lead on the target downrange, you'll be fine, the weapon systems will survive, and you won't unintentionally kill anyone.

Riding the lightning makes you feel fear, followed by uncertainty, ending in euphoria. Your subconscious, which wants to protect you, will tell you to break the ammo belt. But pausing to reload will kill momentum. Focusing on what you need to do and aiming your weapon in the right direction will keep the momentum flowing. This keeps your mind engaged at peak levels and, even better, boosts adrenaline to highs you rarely experience.

I again learned the importance of momentum early in infantry training. I was leading my platoon up a mountain en route to conduct a raid. The tight wedge formation fell apart, so we moved into a column that moved like an accordion. I became concerned that some of the platoon might not make it up the mountain, so we set up our 360-degree security and took a five-minute break—something that earned me a serious ass-chewing from the instructor.

After I made that decision, the instructor explained to me that you never want to lose momentum when climbing up the side of a mountain. In fact, he said, momentum doesn't only apply to going up hills, it applies to leadership. Once you have momentum as a leader, it's important to keep it going. Stopping could cause all momentum to cease. And in the case of a malfunctioning machine gun, the barrel may turn blue from the heat, but it probably won't melt.

As noted in Chapter 7, on risk, a tactical pause presents the opportunity to slow down and reassess. However, a tactical pause rarely provides any benefit halfway up a mountain.

Riding the momentum is easier said than done. When it

seems your company achieves a runaway growth period, your psychological impression may differ from reality. Some leaders become so scared when their flywheel starts working that they sabotage their growth. The fearful leader who spent years trying to achieve this exact high-speed growth is now cowering in the corner debating whether to tell the team to halt. The leader who appointed a captain of the ship and pointed the direction is now second-guessing the captain who got the team to the exact destination the leader plotted.

It is in this very moment we realize a leader's vision means nothing if the leader lacks the courage to see it through. The leader must not only have a vision of growth and preach its virtues to the team but also prepare for growth and be ready for it. Because growth is rarely symmetrical, the leader must build the underdeveloped parts of the company up to speed during periods of rapid growth without halting operations.

More importantly, the leader should prepare to become the next-level version of herself, riding the lightning to a higher level of leadership. For example, if your company grosses $100,000 a year and in five years you want to gross $10 million, you must recognize that not only will your team need to grow their capabilities by a hundred times in five years, but you must grow as a leader at the same rate. You will not be the leader of a $10 million company until you are ready to lead a $10 million company. The problems a $100,000 company faces are much different from the problems a $10 million company faces.

Some of the actions you took to get to $100,000 will destroy your company at $10 million. If you do become the leader of a larger organization before you have developed as a leader, you will likely fail. It would be no different than promoting a 2LT directly to COL. We've all seen leaders who lack the maturity and experience to lead their teams at the next level. Their plight is similar to that of lottery winners who go from broke to millionaires only to be broke again in a couple of years because they lacked the skills to manage the money they won.

This does not mean you should not ride the lighting. To the contrary: proactively prepare to grow as a leader faster than the rate at which you plan to grow the organization. From a survivability and sustainability perspective, it's better to be a $10 million leader of a $100,000 company than to be a $100,000 leader of a $10 million company.

I've seen nine-figure companies with the leadership and infrastructure that make me wonder how they got there and, even more importantly, how they have not crumbled. I have also seen seven-figure companies with leadership, structure, and systems that blow my mind. I can't figure out why they are not even more successful. Sometimes it's the industry, the product, or the location of the business. The size of the company's revenue does not tell the whole story.

As leaders, we often feel frustrated when we can't figure out why some companies outperform us. "We're better than them, execute better, have a more talented team, have superior systems, and have a more mature organizational structure. Yet our competitors are growing at a faster rate and are making more money than us. What are we doing wrong? Where am I, as a leader, failing?" Sometimes the answer is that the other company rode the lighting when it struck and you didn't. Or, in the optimistic alternative, your opportunity to ride the lighting is just around the corner.

THE ONE EXCEPTION

There is one exception to the rule of riding the lightning, and that is to avoid unsafe acts.

In the army, I learned this lesson while a sister company conducted Bradley Table XII, which is where Bradley Fighting Vehicles fire at targets downrange and then the soldiers dismount, exit the back of the vehicle, and clear a trench. During that time, a junior soldier failed to properly clear his M249 inside the trench and, as a result, killed the eighteen-year-old private standing next to him.

If it is safer to break the belt than it is to ride the lightning; know that before you man the weapon. Be aware of your surroundings and risks; don't let the adrenaline make the decision for you.

Within civilian companies, during times of great prosperity, parts of the business gain momentum more rapidly than expected. Periods of exponential growth can seem out of control altogether. The key is to maintain composure and the appearance of control. Keep focused on the proverbial targets downrange, and don't worry about the rate of growth unless you feel you will run out of ammo (cash).

You as the leader will be the only one who can make the split-second decision on whether to ride the lightning or break the belt. Luckily, the military has taught you to be a leader and to think on your feet.

A perfect example is the weapons range. Anybody can yell "cease fire" if they see an unsafe act taking place. Rank doesn't matter. If those words are yelled by a private, the highest-ranking officer will stop what they are doing. Acting quickly and confidently is of the utmost importance. Everyone on your team must feel empowered to speak up if they feel the organization is engaging in dangerous activity. Their willingness to do so usually depends on the culture established by the leader. In organizations with poor cultures, team members engage in wasteful or dangerous behaviors in passive-aggressive ways because someone in a position of authority "told me to do so" even though they knew it was wrong. Individual responsibility should always trump rank and egos. When you empower your team to do what is morally, ethically, and legally right, you can ride the lightning with confidence that if something gets off track, your team members will let you know.

Outside of the military, *The Toyota Way* by Jeffrey Liker offers a relatable lesson here.[1] The book outlines the assembly process of the car manufacturer, Toyota. They have thousands of people working on assembly lines throughout their factories, and anybody can hit the stop button at any given moment. If an employee, regardless of rank or tenure, sees a safety issue along the assembly line, they are encouraged to hit that stop button. The entire management team will then come to the spot on the assembly line, assess the situation, and the line will not begin to move again until there has been a resolution.

Toyota instills confidence in all their employees to be leaders and to act decisively and confidently; the military has done the same for you. There will always be times when things seem out of control or when it feels as though something is unsafe (like a runaway weapon). When these situations occur, you can ensure safety by focusing and maintaining your target. You don't want to lose momentum, but when catastrophic disaster is looming, it is time to call cease fire.

So how will you know if you should ride the lighting or stop for what you perceive to be a safety risk or a developing catastrophe? I don't know. You as the leader must make that decision. And the fate of your company will depend on it.

AFTER-ACTION REVIEW

Sustain

1. Momentum comes fast; be ready.

2. Don't stop just because you fear the pace.

3. You must become a leader who can handle runaway growth before it happens; remember the lottery winner problem.

Improve

1. Rapid growth creates new problems. Anticipate problems, and plan to handle them before they materialize.

2. Maintain focus downrange.

3. Know that momentum may abruptly halt, and prepare accordingly.

9

PREPARE FOR INSPECTION!

Nothing succeeds like the appearance of success.

—Christopher Lasch, *The Culture of Narcissism*

"Open ranks, march!"

I hate military inspections. It all started my junior year in high school when I attended the New Mexico Military Institute. I wanted to focus on football and grades, and I spent my little free time working on both. The structure of military school does not allow much free time because, unfortunately, a lot of your time gets sucked into inspections and preparing for inspections.

We prepared for daily room inspections, daily uniform inspections at breakfast and dinner, and once a month we spent Saturday mornings going through formal inspections of our uniforms, rooms, and M1 rifles. The cadre called every "fault" found during an inspection a "gig." Smudged collar brass—gig. Military creases in your shirt not properly aligned—gig. Shave not close enough—gig. And then the rooms. Shirts in your wall locker not perfectly folded—gig. Hospital corners on your bunk not tight enough—gig. Dust on your windowsill—gig.

I later learned from many drill sergeants that in any inspection, if they were looking for a "discrepancy," they could find ten before even looking at a recruit or walking into a barracks. While I certainly hated wasting time preparing for and suffering through inspections, I also despised the frustration of believing I had done something right only to be told I had failed. While I failed some inspections for legitimate reasons, I failed others because of the sheer pettiness of the inspector. For some inspections, when I missed something obvious, I felt as though I had been given the answers to the test and still failed. My biggest problems with inspections came from me taking the feedback as a personal attack. Today I don't take negative feedback personally, but as a young leader I took everything personally.

The biggest obstacle to effective inspections in any organization is to ensure that the team understands that an inspection is not done *to* them; it's done *for* them. Whether your inspections are planned and documented on a public calendar or are surprise inspections, team members become scared and skeptical. If they go into an inspection feeling this way, they usually come out feeling betrayed or belittled.

As a military leader, you hear stuff like "Inspect what you expect" and "What gets inspected is what gets done." Unfortunately, unless your predecessor provided you with a checklist, you have to decide what to inspect. You can't inspect everything. Not only do you not have enough time, but doing so is micromanaging. Ultimately, for any team to succeed, leaders must be able to trust their subordinates to do their jobs to standard. However, the reason why inspections are paramount to success is that even your best team members have substandard performances from time to time, and we all have deficiencies that we are unaware of.

Also, in times of chaos, things tend to slip through the cracks, if not fall apart completely. You must regularly inspect your systems and team member performance.

PCIS AND PCCS

In the military, precombat inspections (PCIs) and precombat checks (PCCs) ensured that we started every mission prepared. Whether we were rolling out of the wire or humping out of a patrol base, we ensured that our weapons functioned properly, all our gear was securely tied down, logistical support was accounted for, communications devices were tested, and everyone on the team understood our mission and their role. We became so efficient at PCIs and PCCs that the entire process took less than ten minutes. And anyone on the team, regardless of rank, could freely announce any problem to the team.

As your organization scales, multiple leaders will conduct inspections in multiple areas of the business. Your head of IT will be testing your systems to ensure their security. Sales leaders will ensure the sales team follows standard operating procedures. Your HR leader will be inspecting for compliance issues. While your leaders might do a great job inspecting their teams right now, what happens when the leader leaves the organization, goes on vacation, or takes on an all-consuming project? The best teams prepare for the absence of other team members. When it comes to inspections, the best way to prepare is to have inspection checklists.

One of the best books I've read on developing checklists is *The Checklist Manifesto* by Atul Gawande.[1] Remember, inspections are about enforcing a standard. Checklists provide the objective, binary standards. While some small business owners may balk at a culture of uniformity, without it, it becomes nearly impossible to track which tasks have been completed and which have not. Checklists simplify the inspection. Either each action on the checklist happened or it didn't.

Of course, inspections go beyond your people and your processes. Inspect your data. In today's business world, some data is worth more than the company that possesses it.

Data is a key ingredient in your decision-making process. You must inspect your data for accuracy and timeliness. Inaccurate and untimely data can be worse than useless—it can be misleading. It's also important to structure your data! It could be the most valuable part of your business, and if you don't structure it correctly and you can't quickly access it in an easily digestible format, you won't be able to harness its true power in your organization.

I have missed countless opportunities because I did not have my data structured for quick retrieval. At one point, after consulting an engineer, I discovered the cost and time involved in restructuring our data would be massive, so I put it off. Big mistake. I had great data for my individual clients in their individual files, but holistically, our data was not structured in a way to allow us to spot trends in our industry or our performance. It took us years to unravel the data into a system that could be easily inspected and understood.

Put simply, data should be organized so that you can find key information effortlessly. As an analogy from the military, consider my first Bradley Table VIII gunnery. After spending the night in our vehicles, the battalion commander walked by and said, "I'd like to see the load plan for your company." I looked at the makeshift camp between our vehicles—the Bradleys with their ramps down; exposed MRE trash on the floor of the vehicles; poncho liners stuffed in containers designated for other equipment; ammo cans in the grass, which could have been empty or full; and socks drying on top of the vehicle.

The problem was not the unprofessional appearance but rather the disorganization, which made it difficult to locate ammunition, tools, gear, equipment, and weapons. If you remember pristine change of command inspection readiness, this was the opposite.

Your data should look like a change-of-command inspection: you've ensured 100 percent accountability of all equipment, which is neatly organized and easy to locate. Otherwise, the outgoing commander is going to receive a statement of charges for the missing items, which he will gladly pass along to the junior soldier holding the hand receipt for those items. If you can't find something you need buried in your unstructured data, it's like looking for a thumb drive (now forbidden) in a

Not prepared for inspection

postdeployment connex. Sure, you may eventually find it, but you will be digging for quite some time.

INSPECTIONS WITHOUT SURPRISES

As a cadet at Fort Knox, I remember hearing drill sergeants talk about our next day's inspection like it was Christmas. The drill sergeants couldn't wait for all the surprises we cadets had for them, and since Christmas is the season of giving, they assured us that they had many "gifts" for us if we didn't pass the inspection.

When you play the role of inspector or auditor within your own organization, inspections seem like the opposite of Christmas morning. Instead of joyfully rushing into a room to unwrap gifts you've dreamed about for months, you anxiously search for things you hope you won't find. Usually, the person or organization getting inspected knows their deficiencies and hopes the inspector won't find them. Instead of presenting the inspector with gifts, they hope the inspector does not see the brightly colored Easter eggs hidden in the tall weeds of the business.

While the real value in conducting inspections is that they help the organization see what is not readily apparent, any information that should be easily accessible to every member of the organization must be. For years, I conducted quarterly and annual employee performance reviews. Inevitably, a handful of nonperformers would balk at their performance metrics and claim that the metrics "must be wrong" or that they had no idea they were underperforming. After a couple years, I figured out that the problem was not the underperformers, the problem was that I, as the leader, was not being as transparent with the numbers.

No, I didn't obfuscate the data, but I failed to provide it regularly enough to give the team actionable feedback. My first step to fix this was to email each team member a weekly scorecard with red and green numbers. Green numbers meant the team member had hit the target for that metric. Red numbers meant the team member had failed to hit the metric for that week.

My top performers loved the weekly scorecards. They strived to hit all green every week. Low performers hated the scorecards and after a few weeks stopped looking at them. During our first quarterly performance review after launching the scorecard, I asked a low performer, "Joe," whether he reviewed his scorecard every week. Joe defensively said, "Yes, I look at it every week." I then asked, "On a scale of one to ten, how would you rate yourself, Joe?" He enthusiastically replied, "Eight." I then pulled out a stack of his twelve weekly scorecards and placed them on the table. "So based on these scorecards, you are an eight out of ten, Joe? Would you care to review these?" Joe stared at the stack of scorecards and then looked me in the eyes. "I'm a five." I didn't have the courage to tell him the truth, which would have been, "You're not a five on your best day." Instead, I asked Joe if he wanted to do better. Joe lied and said he wanted to improve. The following week I put Joe on a performance improvement plan (PIP), and the next week he quit.

My purpose behind the scorecards was not to make underperformers like Joe quit, but to provide timely, transparent feedback so any team member failing to meet the standards could take timely corrective action. Performance reviews with my top performers that quarter went well, but they were not satisfied with only seeing their scorecard. One of my top performers, Stephanie, asked, "How do I know how I am performing against my peers?" I responded, "You're crushing it; why do you care how everyone else is performing?" Stephanie gave me a cold look. "Because I need to know if I'm the best." By the time I completed quarterly performance counseling, my top performers echoed Stephanie's concern. They didn't just want transparency into their numbers, they wanted transparency into everyone's numbers.

Would I provide the team access to a consolidated scorecard, where team members could compare their numbers to their peers? I struggled with this request for a day. On one hand, I did not want to shame underperformers for fear of alienating them and losing any opportunity I had to help them achieve the standard. On the other hand, my duty to my high performers was to make them even better. High performers, by nature, maintain hypercompetitiveness. My high performers wanted to compete with each other. I sought the counsel of my leadership team and wound up split on the issue.

Ultimately, my decision would come down to organizational values. On the one hand, if I wanted to maintain a harmonious atmosphere that encouraged teamwork and made everyone feel safe and valued regardless of contribution, I could not make everyone's numbers public. The public scorecards would likely drive a rift between the high performers and the underperformers. I could lose loyal team members who had poured their hearts into supporting the team. Team members who willingly sacrificed so much for the team might feel betrayed by a leader who exposed their naked underperformance. But what did my tolerance of their underperformance say about me as their leader? Wasn't the leader's job to get everyone to the standard? Would scorecards revealing underperformers expose me as a weak leader?

I ultimately chose to support the high performers because that decision better aligned with promises I had made to the organization. I had promised the team a bigger, better, higher-paying future where they would work with the best talent. I preached accountability and transparency. If we chose to not show performance metrics because we might hurt the feelings of underperformers, where would it stop? Would we halt our inspections because they might turn up deficiencies and bruise a team member's ego?

Just as I feared, the team scorecards offended the underperformers and their allies while invigorating our champions. Our best performers became even more competitive, and our worst performers got worse. Leaders pulled me aside to persuade me to change the policy. Several team members quit. At the end of the year, turnover was at an all-time high, but so were profits and bonus payments to high performers. Not only did our high performers have their best financial year, but we also didn't lose a single high performer.

Within a year, the effectiveness of the scorecards began to dissipate. The competitors grew restless, wanting to beat the different metrics of the business's other sections. Instead of just emailing weekly scorecards to each section, we decided to also post real-time data on large eighty-inch screens throughout all non-client-facing parts of the office known as "scoreboards" and "leaderboards." While some of the scores on the leaderboard remained section specific, other metrics were firmwide. Now any team member could see all our key performance indicators in real time with direct attribution to the individual team member responsible for the win. You can't walk down a hall or stop in a breakroom without seeing the leaderboards. Even though we've had these screens up for years now, I still find employees transfixed by them, waiting for the next updated slide to pop up.

On occasion, we failed to inspect the data that we posted on the leaderboards, and our top performers called us out to the team. I cannot overstress the importance of accurate data when posting leaderboards. If your data is wrong, the leadership team loses credibility, and the great impact the leaderboard has on your culture will decompose into distrust. Publicly posting inaccurate data happens from time to time, but we remain vigilant in ensuring any data discrepancies are fixed immediately.

PUSH DATA; DON'T EXPECT A PULL

I believe our success behind the public scorecards, scoreboards, and leaderboards came not from making the information available to everyone on the team but from pushing it to them. Your best performers focus on what they need to win. They have no time to log into another system and search for the metrics you want to show them. Furthermore, in the rare event they log on to another system, they don't have the patience to conduct a scavenger hunt to find the metrics. You must push the information to them, not just tell them where to look.

Several units I served with in the active army and the National Guard loved to put everything on the "AKO sharedrive." If you needed a template, a slide deck, a memorandum, or any other work product, no one ever sent an attachment; they just responded, "It's on the shared drive." Then, after spending hours on the shared drive bouncing from information point to information point like a sadistic land-nav course, you determined you couldn't find it.

If you want someone to use data, give it to them; don't tell them where to find it. One important lesson I learned when I begrudgingly transitioned from an infantry officer to a logistician was the difference between "push" and "pull." In planning logistics, it's often advantageous to push logistics to the frontline units rather than to wait for unit requests. As a logistician, I learned to forecast the needs of others, and my job was to know what the units needed before they requested it. I had to procure logistical support long before the unit actually needed it. Furthermore, units outside the wire may not have the luxury of sending logistics reports and requests on time if they are actively engaged with the enemy. And there was always the possibility that an inexperienced unit executive officer lacked the knowledge to request what his unit really needed to complete the mission. I had to inspect those requests and often supplement them with what the unit truly needed.

In short, when you push information rather than wait for others to pull it, you are more likely to get people to pay attention to it. The entire point of conducting an inspection of metrics—or an inspection of anything else—is to get that information to the person who created the result so they can use it to improve. Inspections find faults and discrepancies in search of getting better results, not placing blame. The easier you make it for someone to get the information about their errors, the more time and effort they can spend on getting the results you desire.

INSPECT YOUR PROCESSES

Finally, don't just inspect your metrics. Inspect your processes to ensure they are being followed. When you stop inspecting functional areas and only start looking when the metrics drop, the team knows it. For some reason, our sales process needs to be inspected every couple of weeks so that it does not take on a life of its own. For some companies, this means listening to sales calls. For others, this means having each salesperson simply walk them through the steps. Spoiler alert: most don't follow the SOP.

You must inspect website content, financial records, employment records, and so forth. You're not just looking for data discrepancies but to find out whether the processes you put in place are being followed. There are few things more frustrating than spending days drafting a process and weeks training on it and implementing it, only to learn six months later that nobody follows it.

INSPECT YOUR VENDORS

Inspect what your vendors are doing. Many times I failed well-meaning vendors because I did not inspect their work. It seems simple: you pay someone to do a job for you, and you make sure they do it correctly. Unfortunately, even the most reputable vendors need your direction and guidance to fulfill your vision and meet your standards. When you set standards and provide early feedback, you get better results. The hours you spent negotiating the contract and trading papers back and forth to develop acceptable statements of work (SOW) and master service agreements (MSA) won't be enough to ensure their work aligns with your vision. You must inspect their work and provide feedback just as you do for any employee.

When I deployed to Bosnia in 1999, it seemed we dealt with few contractors. My impression as a young lieutenant was that one contractor, Haliburton or "KBR," was the contractor that ran all contracted logistics and operated silently in the background of the military, just like contractors like Raytheon who developed our weapons systems. Six years later in Iraq, I noticed contractors everywhere. Many of those contractors, third-country nationals (TCNs), seemed to operate autonomously. Some of those contractors appeared competent; others appeared blatantly ineffective. The contractors didn't operate under our rules, and the rumor mill produced information that contractors provided soldiers with alcohol, drugs, and prostitutes.

Unfortunately, as a civilian, vetting contractors can be difficult. Many vendors appear to spend a lot more time on dialing in their marketing materials and sales pitches than delivering quality products and services. Even after you check references and conduct research on vendors, you may still wind up with their "C Team," which will provide inferior service compared to their "A Team." While some established and well-meaning vendors might not have the bandwidth to achieve the standards they promise your organization, your inspections may reveal other vendors as incompetent or fraudsters.

I've been burned most often in marketing and technology. I failed to conduct deep research on certain companies because I wanted their sales pitches to be true. When I saw a marketing firm with great advertising content, I assumed that if their designers and copywriters could produce amazing content for their own company, they had the talent to take our image to the next level. Later, I learned that the marketing company had hired an outside agency.

One area where you must constantly inspect vendor work is in content building. You as the leader must protect your brand. If you run a growing company, you produce marketing content that lives on the web in search engines and on social media. Finding a partner to help you develop quality content can lead to explosive growth. Unfortunately, you must constantly inspect that content to protect your brand. Poorly written and inaccurate content makes your company look incompetent and lazy—even if your vendor created it.

It's not always a bad sign if marketing content appears substandard in the first iteration. You must show the vendor exactly where they are failing and exactly what you expect. Show, don't tell—and remember, the content is you! You, as the leader of the organization, are the protector of the brand. If you don't read what your vendors put out as you, then you are failing to inspect. If, after your inspection and feedback, the vendor fails to improve, exit that relationship as soon as practical. If the vendor won't respect your inspections in feedback in the honeymoon phase of the relationship, they will never strive to meet your company's high standards and you will never trust them.

As a new 2LT, I remember bringing a memorandum to my company commander for signature. While the document was well written and clear, I had messed up on the formatting, and the document failed to conform with Army Regulation 25-50. After a five-minute ass-chewing, the commander taught me a lesson I had to learn over and over again: Review every document before you sign it or approve it. Your signature is your credibility; don't sign anything that is not excellent. The same goes for allowing vendors to publish blogs, videos, or anything else under your brand. Though it is painful to inspect, the inspection needs to be done by a competent member of your team. Ideally, you delegate this to a highly talented team member, but if you delegate to the wrong person, it's your brand and credibility on the line.

One mistake I made with vendor-generated content was, after seeing a horribly written blog and spending an hour editing it, I failed to ensure that the vendor published the edited version. Not only did I lose an hour of my life editing, but I lost a ton of credibility when that vendor posted their original substandard version. The article was not only inaccurate; it was offensive. I received emails, text messages, and even got tagged in social media posts with screenshots of the offensive post. While I am perfectly fine receiving mass criticism for my opinions, this blog was not my opinion. Fortunately, the blog was so horribly written that even social media commentators cried foul and said, "This is so poorly written it doesn't seem real."

Inspecting your technology vendors may be more complicated, but at its core, the concept is the same. I'm ashamed to say that I allowed one company to sell me a product that didn't yet exist, and it took me half a year of talking with their engineers and my assigned "project manager" to learn the company lacked the ability to produce the product the salesperson had promised me. When I explained the situation to a former G6 in the army, he just laughed and said, "That's what we call 'vaporware.' It doesn't exist. That company pulled one over on you."

But even competent technology vendors need accountability.

Tech projects must stay on timelines, and vendors must deliver as promised. Often you won't know whether your tech vendor is performing unless you set performance measures and inspect against them. If you lack the knowledge base to hold your tech vendors accountable, you may want to hire an in-house tech expert to handle the tech vendor accountability.

INSPECT YOUR PROCEDURES AND EXPECT TO UPDATE THEM

Inspect your procedures. One of my greatest frustrations comes when well-meaning members of an organization create additional, unnecessary policies and procedures that choke out efficiency. This happened to our sales process.

Several months after implementing a new sales system, I couldn't figure out why so many leads were stuck in our pipeline. Even though we followed a training program, every single team member gave a different answer for how they were handling incoming cold calls. I sent an email to the managers asking for the policy or procedure they were using. Not a single team member provided me a document. Instead, they all crafted contradictory emails explaining how they were doing things. Somehow our entire process had become misaligned. What happened?

We had stopped inspecting the process regularly. Yes, we examined data, but no one was checking to see whether we were following our own procedures. We were missing thousands of dollars in opportunities each day. We thought we were a well-oiled machine because we "knew our numbers" and our data showed we were doing well. However, the data failed to show well-meaning team members' *sua sponte* self-imposed inefficiencies that choked our growth potential.

I remember when the TOW missile system (tube-launched, optically tracked, wire-guided heavy anti-tank missile weapon system) on the Bradley Fighting Vehicle received a wireless upgrade to "TOW FF," advertised as "fire and forget." The message was, once you launched the TOW missile, it would hit the target. You no longer needed to guide the missile after you launched it. After two years, the plan failed, and the TOW FF disappeared.

When it comes to systems, there is no "fire and forget." We had developed a great sales system, but without regular inspections, entropy had set in, and well-meaning team members began adjusting the system without understanding the consequences. The harsh lesson learned was that great system implementation will not stick without regular system inspection.

The other reason to constantly inspect your systems is to capitalize on opportunities to improve them. No system is futureproof. Sometimes an advancement in technology makes changes necessary. Years ago, many organizations struggled to go paperless because they failed to modernize their systems. Recently, companies struggled to implement remote work. Getting the technology in place proved to be a false summit—where leaders failed was in inspecting the productivity of their newly remote teams. Our current challenge is in implementing artificial intelligence, AI, into our systems. While vendors flaunt their AI capabilities as a way to "exponentially" increase productivity, if you fail to inspect the AI work, you may find that the only thing your vendors have exponentially created is garbage. Failing to adequately inspect AI work could ruin your reputation. Innovation always requires inspection.

Laws and regulations may change your systems. Your competitors, rising costs, or manpower issues can all render your once-superior systems obsolete. While you need systems to run any business, you must constantly innovate to make better systems. But how do you know when you need to innovate? You inspect. Your inspections tell you if your systems are working correctly. When you discover that your systems are no longer operating correctly or are no longer getting excellent results, you innovate and build a new system.

"THE BALLOON COULD GO UP AT ANY TIME"

I remember a sergeant major telling us that military orders could pull us away from our families at any point. The string attaching us to our lives could sever at any moment, removing us from one reality and throwing us into a new one.

When the deployment comes, soldiers tend to take inspections more seriously. In garrison, it seems inspections are all about compliance, but the army trains its soldiers that the difference between a standard and substandard inspection is life and death. Ideally, we diligently inspect, but when the atmospheric conditions of our operating environment change, we feel the heat. The inspections become more important.

Preparing to deploy

When the team knows the gravity of the situation, they understand their inspections affect team members they may never meet. Consider the parachute rigger. The rigger packs chutes for soldiers who will jump. The airborne soldier trusts that whoever inspected the rigger's work did it right. But, just to be safe, we jump with a reserve chute, which was also inspected.

DAILY APPEARANCE, THE INFORMAL INSPECTION

As a young infantry lieutenant, I didn't believe real soldiers cared about starched uniforms and shined boots. In my mind, that was basic training and ROTC toy soldier stuff. My first day as a brand-new platoon leader in Fort Hood, I showed up in an unpressed battle dress uniform (BDU) with dull, brush-shined jungle boots. Perfectly dressed for army training in the field. The problem is that my unit was not in the field, we were in a garrison environment.

When I met my new right hand, my platoon sergeant, SFC Ray Kaloplastos, I noticed his crisp-pressed BDUs looked harder than woodpecker lips. His smooth, shined boots could have been made of wet black glass. His flawless uniform displayed almost every possible badge or patch you could earn in the army: drill sergeant, expert infantry badge, airborne, air assault, pathfinder.

Kaloplastos looked disappointed to see me. "LT, we're in red cycle. We don't go to the field for another two weeks," he said.

According to our training schedule, we would be preparing to conduct Bradley Gunnery Table VIII soon, and I saw no reason to spend $3.25 to get my uniform "professionally starched" to spend a day in the motor pool. I also believed that spit-shining boots designed for combat and breaking brush in jungles and wooded areas made no sense.

Kaloplastos continued in a drill-sergeant-like cadence, "In garrison, soldiers shine boots and press uniforms. Your uniform looks like you pulled it right out of a duffel bag. Your boots look like they were shined with a chocolate bar. Around

here we dress like professional soldiers. Around here we lead
by example."

SFC Kaloplastos's high-and-tight haircut could not hide his
head turning red above his ears. Kaloplastos didn't seem excited to
introduce me, their new rag bag LT, to his platoon. The redness
filling the sides of his head came from embarrassment, not anger.

Let me be perfectly clear, I chose to become an infantry
officer because I wanted to lead soldiers into battle to support
and defend the constitution of the United States. I became an
officer to lead America's best in the worst conditions. I did not
swear a solemn oath and commit years of my life to the army
because I wanted to look pretty in a uniform. Scuffed boots and
wrinkled camouflage didn't bother me.

Twenty-four hours later at morning formation I appeared in
freshly starched BDUs and highly shined boots. I looked like
I had jumped right out of AR 670-1 (the army's uniform standards manual). SFC Kaloplastos saved me the embarrassment
of looking like a dirtbag at my first formation with the first
military unit I would ever lead.

I soon learned as a green, inexperienced 2LT, I could control
only three things: my individual readiness, my attitude, and the
neatness of my uniform. Leading without experience becomes
even more difficult when you don't look like a leader. My first
ninety days with the unit, I was as useless as wet toilet paper,
but at least I didn't look like it.

Sergeants know that uniformity and consistency are key
to executing a mission. Superior execution at scale requires
standardization. In the field, every soldier keeps their first-aid

pouch in the same place on their kit so if they are injured, their buddy knows precisely where to find their field dressing. All soldiers pack their rucksacks with the same packing list so that if you need something out of your or anyone else's ruck to aid in mission completion, you know it's there. All Bradley Fighting Vehicles maintain the same load plan, so the interiors of the vehicles look identical throughout the battalion. You can execute much more rapidly when you know where to find stuff.

Not every soldier maintains the same pride in appearance, which accounts for the differences inside a formation. But here's why inspecting appearance can be just as important as inspecting functionality: Think about how your brain reacts to a person with dirty hands and disheveled hair who dresses in wrinkled clothes. We assume anyone with this appearance must be homeless. We all knew a soldier who showed up to formation like this. They were a mess. Unprofessional. Not the qualities you desired in a battle buddy, or the type of person you wanted watching your back downrange.

While sometimes the cleanest-looking soldiers are the biggest dirtbags and the dirtiest-looking soldiers are the best tactical athletes, most people assume that those who don't take pride in their appearance usually don't take pride in anything else they do. When we see someone who appears sloppy and unprofessional, we judge. Those judgments influence decisions. And those decisions can influence careers. Think back on your own experience. Did you ever meet someone who looked like a slob? Did your initial impression ever completely subside? Did you ever walk into a messy office and assume: this person must be disorganized and incompetent? Uniformity creates an environment where looking good also creates efficiency. In military motor pools, soldiers park vehicles online—ready to execute.

Your appearance matters because it proves functionality. That's why we keep our weapons and equipment clean and maintained. Inspections matter. Barracks inspections, weapon inspections, and uniform inspections—they all matter. Inspections ensure equipment is functioning properly and in good working order. The same can be said about you and your appearance.

APPEARANCES DON'T DECEIVE

Taking pride in the way you maintain yourself goes much further than appearance. It's about more than a clean haircut and pressed clothes. Maintaining the tools we use in our everyday lives has the same effect. We conduct preventive maintenance checks and services (PMCS) on our vehicles to ensure they work properly and protect the gear we will need in the field.

You have the freedom to choose how you appear, and you should be focusing on the first impression people will have on you. That applies to a job interview, a first date, a business partnership, and anything else. Your appearance can either help or hinder your ability to move forward.

Appearance can be more important in the civilian sector than the military. Everyone judges your appearance, every day. In the military, if you don't look the part, a sergeant will tell you and may even make you do push-ups for looking like a soup sandwich.

Civilians see you looking like a slob and readily assume that's who you are. If you're a leader and your team looks like slobs, you're a slob too. What your drill sergeant didn't tell you is that after basic training, when you report to a real military unit, if you look like a slob, he looks like a slob too. That's why military units still hold uniform inspections. It's not just about the individual but the climate the commander sets.

Imagine you need to hire a lawyer for the most important issue in your life. You need to hire someone to protect your future. You show up at a law office and the lawyer greets you in a dirty T-shirt, cargo shorts, and flip-flops. He hasn't shaved in a few days, has greasy hair, and is bleary eyed. The guy looks and smells like he partied in Panama City last night. Do you trust him?

As the leader, you set the command climate for your organization. Years ago, a former marine joined our organization, not as an attorney but in a support role position. No one expected this Marine Corps veteran to wear a suit to work, and no one asked him to do so. Yet he showed up every day wearing a suit and tie. For the first week, his coworkers poked fun at him for "trying to look like a lawyer." Within a month, every marine veteran in our office wore a suit and tie. Within the next ninety days, most of the army veterans wore a blazer and tie. Suddenly the army and marine veterans began making fun of the navy and air force veterans for looking unprofessional in their khaki pants and polo shirts.

This is where it gets good. Once the uniform standards improved, professionalism throughout the organization changed.

Everyone started dressing better and acting more professional in meetings, and our productivity increased. People in uniform not only look powerful; they feel empowered.

I am sure some readers will claim what they wear to work doesn't matter. They will tell you they prefer a relaxed dress code or that they are more productive wearing jeans and a T-shirt. They will cite the Steve Jobs mock turtleneck or the Zuckerburg T-shirt or Silicon Valley hoodies. If that is the uniform you choose for your organization, that's great. Know that the impression you choose is the impression your potential customers see. If you prefer a relaxed dress code or relaxed work hours, don't be surprised when you experience relaxed standards. I am less interested in what's cool, in style, or trending than I am in what works.

No doubt, people who dress the part, feel the part. If you suffer from imposter syndrome, know this: looking professional not only makes you feel more professional but makes others in the room feel your professionalism. A quick uniform inspection, which may mean looking in the mirror or asking a buddy to check you before a meeting, can either help or hinder your one shot at a first impression. First impressions last forever.

INSPECT YOUR APPEARANCE ONLINE AND IN PRINT

Appearance goes beyond physical presence. I often make my first impression with my writing. If the document I send lacks clarity, contains grammatical errors, uses a silly font, or is devoid of organizational structure, I appear unprofessional. In fact, at this point, I might as well add emojis to my document to remove all doubt about my incompetence. I may be impeccably dressed, but the person reading my documents only sees a disorganized, lazy, dumb person who lacks the education, intelligence, and self-respect to write a coherent, professionally styled thought on a piece of paper or email. People you never meet in person judge you by your work product. If it's bad, don't worry; they will never agree to meet you.

In today's digital world, your online appearance can be just as important. I hear lamentations regularly from seasoned professionals who can't get business. They possess all the skills, experience, and accomplishments, but their phones don't ring, no one fills out their web forms, and despite paying tons of money for web traffic each month, nobody seems to be interested in hiring them. Then I check out their website, their web biography, or the online directories in which they are listed. With the photograph from 1998, the lack of accomplishments listed in the past two decades, no testimonials, and no online reviews, I wouldn't hire them either. Do you even care about your career? Sure, you cultivated referral sources, but a referral no longer guarantees a hire. The referral will check you out online before they decide whether to call you, even when the person they trust most referred them to you.

Having an ate-up website or incomplete biography is the digital equivalent of showing up to formation looking like dirt. At first glance, and you only get one glance, your online presence screams what you lack. A closer examination reveals spelling errors, contradictions, a message that fails to resonate with anyone, and no call to action.

Immediately after a prospective client or customer reads your online biography, if they are still interested in hiring you, they investigate your social media. Do you have a presence on every social media channel? I hear a ton of excuses about how social media is "personal." It's not. You can change your privacy settings, but social media companies will find a way to use your data. So don't fight it; use it as a tool. Look and act like a professional on social media.

Who is most likely to refer business to you? Friends and family. Who is on your social media? Friends and family. Clean up your page, stay away from politics and negativity, and look like you are prepared for an in-ranks inspection. Because whether you decide to post curated professional pictures or casual shots, people inspect your image. In social media, you control your appearance and your message, so make it something positive.

Take pride in your appearance online and offline. Once a consumer has a first impression of you, it will be almost impossible to change it. Think back to when you were a kid. Did you prefer Coke or Pepsi? If you had one dollar back then, which would you buy? If you would buy Coke, how hard would it be to convince you to start buying Pepsi? If your first online impression doesn't make you the obvious choice, you've lost that sale, forever.

The growth of your business will be limited by the quality of people you hire. Your prospective hires are not only checking out your company on job sites like Indeed and Glassdoor but also looking at your company profile on LinkedIn, as well as your individual profile. They scour your website and read online reviews about you and your team. If you don't keep your digital world inspection-ready, you will fail their inspection and lose their trust before you even meet.

Think about how many people inspect your digital appearance every day for the first time. Check out the Google analytics for your website, and you will see how many new people look at you every day.

Remember that consumers have a voice. As a young officer, I learned quickly that the enemy always has a vote when it comes to operations. The consumer is your friend, not your enemy, but the consumer has a similar vote and the opportunity to make that vote public through online reviews. Back in 2016, I attended a conference in Las Vegas and learned about the importance of online reviews. Like most lawyers, I thought the presentation didn't apply to us. I knew all about the "Amazon effect" and how people trust online reviews, but I dismissed the concept as irrelevant to my industry.

When I returned from the conference, I noticed we didn't have many reviews, and it seemed that the only people who left reviews were either really happy with us or really upset. As I dug deeper, I noticed that some of the negative reviews were based on outcomes we could not control, such as the amount of time it took the VA to decide a veterans disability rating decision appeal. Other bad reviews came from people whose cases we had rejected. We even had a review from a person who acknowledged they never did business with us—they just didn't like us.

Like all businesses, we had some negative reviews that we earned. In some instances, we provided excellent legal service, but our customer service was substandard. And of course, nobody wins every case, which can result in disappointed clients. Feedback is a gift, and negative feedback allows you to fix problems. I am grateful for the honest negative reviews and client feedback that help us improve our client service, identify weaknesses, and remove toxic team members. When clients identify problems, you get the opportunity to fix them. Consider the more defenseless position when the client votes with their feet, bad-mouthing you to everyone, but you never find out about the problem and never fix it, only adding to your reputational damage.

When you're the boss, no one is going to write your annual officer evaluation report. No one is going to sit you down for a quarterly counseling session. You don't even have a senior rater. Without a boss, the actionable feedback you receive from clients and employees is priceless. Embrace the suck, find value in the negative experiences, and use those opportunities to improve your organization. Negative reviews also provide accountability. When you fail to meet client expectations, you face the real consequence of a negative review.

While the negative reviews bother all of us, what motivated our team were the positive reviews. Before we started requesting online reviews, we had a few great online reviews, but we had thousands of happy clients. Every month we received multiple thank-you cards from veterans who received six-figure backpay awards. The letters told us how we changed their lives. The letters named team members who had helped them, described their struggles with the VA, wished they had hired us sooner, and loved the fact that we had so many veterans on our team helping them.

Our happy clients offered to bring us vegetables from their gardens, deer jerky, and baked goods. But would they be willing to write an online review? I didn't know; we'd never asked. At first, the concept of asking clients for reviews seemed awkward. However, as we learned, automating the process made it easier. Now, every time we get a positive online review, we email it to the entire team so they can experience our client's gratitude.

You are responsible for the digital appearance of your company. If you fail to capture your wins, accomplishments, and reviews, it's like wearing your Class A uniform without your rank or ribbons. Your online reputation is like a military award: if you earn it, wear it. Your customers will be looking at your website like a promotion packet. Your official photo, experience, awards, and recommendations all matter.

In sum, as much as I hated them in the military, inspections provide the invaluable feedback necessary to improve and grow your team and systems. In today's digital world, the salty drill sergeants are replaced by potential customers who inspect your online presence and reputation. When you fail the customer's inspection, they won't gig you or drop you, they will do something much worse. They will avoid you.

AFTER-ACTION REVIEW

Sustain

1. Your team knows what you inspect.

2. Rehearse, rehearse, rehearse.

3. Correctly performed inspections tell you not only whether the team follows procedures but whether the current procedures are effective.

Improve

1. Your standards may not be clear. If you don't inspect, you won't know.

2. Your data may not be accurate. If you don't inspect, you won't know.

3. Properly conducted inspections can tell you when you need to update your systems.

10

WE DO MORE BY 7:00 A.M. THAN MOST PEOPLE DO ALL DAY

The sergeant is the army.

—Attributed to Dwight D. Eisenhower

The most impressive accomplishments of the United States military occur in the execution of operations. Endless books dissect innovation, strategy, and vision, but the difference between success and failure lies not in these lofty concepts but in the ability to execute and complete tasks to standard. The United States military, the greatest fighting force in the history of the world, wins with superior execution. As Patton said, "A good plan violently executed *now* is better than a perfect plan next week."[1] While historians credit much of America's military successes since World War I to strategies or visions of brilliant general officers, the truth is that wars are won in the trenches, jungles, deserts, and urban areas, not in planning rooms.

Strategy matters, but without grit and fierce execution, strategy is fantasy.

All the KPI, OKI, scorecards, scoreboards, leaderboards, metrics, and tracking software become worthless if your team can't execute. Military teams execute at high levels because sergeants know how to get their teams to execute. What sergeants know about execution has been proven for thousands of years. I've studied fascinating leadership theories, but hollow aspirational thoughts of "leadership experts" never tell you the operational truths that all sergeants know. Books like *Traction* by Gino Wickman, *Scaling Up* by Verne Harnish, and others that follow the Rockefeller habits tell you how to measure and report progress. These tools work well when you have a team that can execute. When your team fails to execute, these tools simply mirror poor results. Excellence materializes in the execution, not the plan.

The noncommissioned officer is the backbone of the United States military. While officers plan, sergeants actually get stuff done. Sergeants know to look beyond the mission statement and study the commander's intent prior to executing any mission.

As a leader, you must provide precise guidance to those who will execute on your plan and ensure they understand the reason they're doing it, in addition to the desired end state. Good sergeants focus on the "why" or "in order to" (IOT) clause of the mission statements and do not waste manpower or resources accomplishing tasks that do not comply with the commander's intent.

Anyone who has served knows sergeants are not just super smart when it comes to executing operations, some are superhuman. If you served long enough, you know dozens of superhuman sergeants. Civilians reading this book probably imagine the sergeant who carried a wounded soldier hundreds of meters under enemy fire to safety. But for those of us who served, we know that one heroic act does not make a sergeant a great leader. What makes sergeants great leaders is that they execute with maniacal focus and technical proficiency every single day, in everything they do. Their uniforms are perfect, they're never late, they're physical fitness gods, they train their soldiers incessantly, they know everything and want to know even more. And these omniscient, omnipotent beings care more about the success of the team and their individual soldiers than most civilians can fathom. If, as a leader, you can explain the IOT to the sergeant, it will be done.

The sergeant who earns the most prestigious awards in combat or garrison impresses everyone except his unit, who already knew he is the best. While we stand in formation at the position of attention listening to the award citation, we all wonder why the chain of command took so long to recognize our sergeant.

FALL IN!

Sergeants own the first formation of the day. At 0530 sergeants show up, full of energy, ensuring all their soldiers are present and in the right uniform. They line their soldiers up with precision. By the end of first formation, soldiers know exactly what must be done today, who must do it, and what standards must be achieved for every task.

Everyone shows up for first formation, every day. In the military, you can't call in sick. You show up for first formation, no matter what. If you are sick, lame, or lazy, you can go to the infirmary during sick call, but not without being excused by your sergeant. If you're really sick, you show up for first formation and your sergeant will ensure you get the medical attention you need. Sergeants even know when soldiers fake illnesses or show up drunk or hungover. When this occurs, sergeants know the soldier really just needs intense physical activity to purge the toxins from their bodies and weakness from their minds. In some instances, after ten minutes of vigorous activity and copious amounts of vomit, the soldier miraculously no longer needs to go to the infirmary.

From time to time, sergeants also conduct random "accountability formations" to account for all personnel and sensitive items. This "show, don't tell" method instills true accountability. The military calls an inaccurate report a "false report," regardless of the culpability of the individual sending the report. Sergeants know accurate reporting means putting eyes and hands on every person and sensitive item.

While "hands on" may seem excessive, it's not. The terrified soldier who lost his night vision device (NODs) and is worried about losing rank, pay, and getting a statement of charges and a letter of reprimand in his personnel file will stuff rocks in his NODs carrying case to hide his failure to maintain accountability of his equipment. Clever as he may be, the soldier cannot outsmart the salty sergeant, who, in formation, orders every soldier to remove their NODs from the carrying case and hold them in their right hand.

Imagine your sergeant holding accountability formations in your civilian organization. Unlike the professional responses of "yes, sergeant" or "no, sergeant," you would hear, "How dare you question the accuracy of my reporting." "I didn't give you permission to touch my company-issued property." "I'm not going to stand in formation, I stand where I want to stand." And this explains the inaccurate reports, lack of accountability, and lack of discipline in most organizations.

Imagine empowering your leaders the way the military empowers its sergeants. I hear business gurus preach about "caring for their employees," but all they talk about is pandering. Give them more benefits: buy them a ping-pong table; give them more vacation days, free lunches, and a three-day workweek; create a sleep room where they can take naps. These actions show you care, right? No, they show incompetence, weakness, and a need to be liked by everyone. These actions don't prove you're a leader, they prove you desire the approval of others more than you desire their success.

Let me tell you about the sergeants and officers who cared about me. They pushed me in physical training until I threw up and then made me do push-ups until I couldn't feel my arms, and then they rolled me onto my back to do flutter kicks until my entire body cramped. They took away my food and my sleep until I began hallucinating. They made me walk tens of miles with blistered and bloodied feet. When I complained my ruck was too heavy, they added ten pounds. When I failed to qualify with my rifle because I am right-handed and left-eye dominant, they made me shoot left-handed at the range for two days straight until I qualified expert. When I wrote a substandard operations order, they made me rewrite it until it was perfect.

If you served, you've experienced this form of love. When your leaders love you so deeply that they would rather break you than see you fail to reach your potential, they have paid you the highest compliment bestowed on mortals. They believe in your potential for greatness, and they express that not in their words but in their relentless dedication to your success.

If you're serious about building a great team, put your leaders in charge of the care, well-being, and performance of their team members as the military does with its sergeants. They show compassion, not through providing comfort, but through relentless challenges that birth capable leaders.

My company has great sergeants. The reality is that I could not lead a team of mediocre sergeants. In business, if you as the leader are mediocre, you will survive. If your sergeants are mediocre, you will stagnate and die. The success of your company lies in the hands of your sergeants. If your HR director is incompetent, you will lose key players, get sued, and your payroll will fall apart. If your CFO is lazy or dishonest, you will face many unnecessary financial hardships. If your marketing director does not analyze the correct data, you will go broke paying for ad spend that generates insufficient qualified leads. If your director of operations ignores your client/customer experience, your lifetime value of a customer will not be worth the acquisition cost. Bottom line, if your subordinate leaders lack the competence and drive to succeed in their roles, you will fail if you tolerate their substandard performance.

APOTHEOSIS: TURNING SOLDIERS INTO SERGEANTS

The military builds sergeants; they don't buy them. The military can buy a civilian with a degree, give them a direct commission, and call them an officer. But you can't buy a sergeant. So how do you make one? In the military, it takes years of experience, developing, mentoring, and training. Finally, after two to four years, the gods of war smile and promote the soldier to join them.

Apotheosis is the Greek word for a mortal's elevation to god status. How is it that some soldiers transform into a non-commissioned officer and others do not? Objectively, every soldier has the same opportunity to become a sergeant, but some choose not to, and others don't have what it takes to become a god.

From my limited perspective as an officer observing junior soldiers rise through the ranks, there seemed to be only two factors that separated the men from the deities. The first was desire: the soldier had to want to be a sergeant, and not just want the rank, but want the burden. The second was attitude: the soldier had to readily soak up knowledge like a sponge, and work like a dog, devoid of ego and full of gratitude.

The soldier, armed with the desire to serve and an impenetrable positive attitude, could not be stopped. Sure, they faced failures, hurdles, and disappointments like all the other soldiers, but they handled themselves differently. They truly believed in their leaders and gathered strength from that belief. It was as if they knew that their leaders believed in them, and so long as they could keep their leaders' faith in them, they could never lose. They knew their leaders had flaws and missteps, but they never breathed a word of it. They sang the company song and seemed to have a Teflon coating to which negativity could not stick.

NCO BUSINESS

As a young officer, I experienced times when I returned to the platoon "cages" (rooms made of fence materials instead of walls) in the back of the company area, which was where the NCOs conducted business, and I was highly encouraged to leave. I would say something stupid like, "What's going on in here, Sergeant? Looks like you guys are having a meeting." In response, the platoon sergeant would cheerfully say, "Hey, Lieutenant, why don't you go get a haircut. We're conducting NCO business." I was either smart enough or foolish enough to avoid saying something stupid like, "What NCO business are you conducting?" Fortunately for me, as 2LT I wore my hair longer than the high and tight you see on most infantry soldiers, so when they told me to get a haircut, I was usually a week or two overdue. I never questioned their "NCO business"; I just got into my POV and drove off base to the barbershop that gave a complimentary shoulder massage with every haircut. When I returned, it appeared the NCOs had successfully completed their business.

One evening, about a month into my first deployment in Bosnia in 1999, I stopped by my platoon sergeant's connex to discuss the next morning's mission. I pounded on the door with no response. I checked the handle and pushed the door open. I observed all my squad leaders, section leaders, and team leaders huddled around my platoon sergeant, who was seated on his bunk wearing his brown BDU undershirt and brown underwear of the same color. At first, I feared these NCOs were planning to frag me; then my insecurities crept in, and a worse fear came over me: maybe they've finally figured out I don't know what the hell I'm doing. They all just stared at me. No one called the room to attention; nobody called me sir. After a few seconds of unbearable silence, I closed the connex door and backed away.

The next day I asked "Sergeant Ski," one of my squad leaders and my workout battle buddy, what they were talking about. Ski just smiled. "NCO business, sir." I finally asked, "What's NCO business?" Ski looked confused, and then his face lit up. "You know everything you need to know about the platoon, and we take care of the stuff you don't need to know about." Ski went on to explain that my role was to plan and lead, and the NCOs' job was to make everything else happen. He said, "Look, officers who get involved in NCO business don't make it. They spend 80 percent of their time trying to do our jobs, and they can't do it. Sir, if we ever need your help, we will ask, and that will probably never happen." Confused, I asked, "But don't I need to know everything that goes on in this platoon?" Ski smiled. "No, sir, you don't. Now add another plate on the squat rack bar."

Learning from SSG Chris Kowalewski in Bosnia

FALLEN ANGELS

One of the most disappointing things we see in the military is the sergeant who goes from superstar to super slug. The invincible, unstoppable, incorruptible sergeant stumbles and doesn't get back up. As leaders, we accept that even the best of us fail from time to time. We occasionally miss the mark, let the team down, or just have a bad day.

When our sergeants have a substandard day, we rarely notice. In fact, they usually agonize over the details of their substandard performance when most of us consider their substandard day better than our best day. However, when their substandard performance becomes more frequent, we know they are facing a challenge greater than any we have experienced. Sometimes their problems stem from their own bad off-duty decisions. Other times, we as leaders unknowingly drag them into hell.

Great sergeants can develop self-destructive habits from failing to confront mental health issues resulting in drinking problems, financial problems, and relationship problems. My experience has been that the sooner a leader addresses personal demons, the sooner they will get back on track. Some of the strongest leaders I know embrace their demons, come to peace with them, and befriend them.

Of course, the strength to overcome your own demons does not mean you should try to partner with someone who cannot overcome their own. One of the saddest moments in leadership is when a promising sergeant chooses the wrong romantic partner and finds themselves crushed under the weight of a dependapotamus who spends all their money, destroys their credit, eats all their food, and siphons off their will to live like a hero. In these circumstances, all we can do is offer our support, make fun of them to their face, and finally have a heart-to-heart conversation about their future.

Conversely, there are times when we as leaders drag our sergeant into hell. We fail to set the example, we micromanage, we strip them of their authority, and we put them in charge of soldiers who lack the desire and authority to become one of them.

For many sergeants, micromanagement is kryptonite. Once we create an environment where we strip them of their authority and decision-making power, they shrivel in an unnatural, restrained leadership construct where we expect them to perform miracles with their hands tied behind their backs. All they can do is watch and cringe until it's too late. They lose their will to perform because they have no one to lead and a supervisor not worth following.

Need results? Team not executing? Anybody can plan; anybody can dream. Few can execute like sergeants.

AFTER-ACTION REVIEW

Sustain

1. Put your plan in writing and let your sergeants execute it.

2. Show the plan, don't just tell the plan, and let your sergeants execute it.

3. Let your sergeants train you.

Improve

1. No plan survives first contact with the enemy, but the enemy will perish if you let your sergeants take charge.

2. Assume your plan is imperfect, and let the team fix the imperfections prior to execution.

3. Proof comes from results, not plans.

11

SHOOT, MOVE, AND COMMUNICATE

Communications without intelligence is noise. Intelligence without communications is irrelevant.

—General Alfred M. Gray, quoted in Otte, *Grayisms*

D o the basic tasks well. You cannot execute the complex until you master the simple. The military taught us the crawl, walk, run methodology. We did not conduct live-fire exercises the first day of training. Before we were allowed to touch a rifle, we learned weapon safety, how to hold a weapon, how to march with a weapon, how to assemble and disassemble a weapon, and how to clean a weapon. We then spent countless hours learning basic rifle marksmanship (BRM) and practiced breathe, relax, aim, squeeze (BRAS) before ever sending a live round downrange. We learned to battlesight zero our rifles, and once we zeroed them, we fired them in a highly controlled environment where all commands came from the range tower, and a swarm of range safeties with their white and red ping-pong paddles monitored our every move until a sergeant "rodded" us off the range.

We also learned the basics of individual movement techniques (IMTs) of high crawl, low crawl, three- to five-second rush, and so forth. After we practiced IMT techniques with rubber rifles, otherwise known as "rubber ducks," we practiced with real weapons with blanks and red and yellow blank firing adapters (BFAs) on the muzzle of our weapons. We trained both day and night so that we could IMT in limited visibility. Then the trainers added live rounds whizzing past us about ten feet above our heads.

Finally, after demonstrating we could move under fire at night, we were allowed to IMT with live ammunition and real rifles and conduct a live-fire training exercise. We combined the skills of shooting and moving, and we shot at targets as we rushed and then crawled toward targets.

The most difficult part of the shoot, move, and communication trinity was the communication. Communicating when you're out of breath and your ears are ringing from the crackle of gunfire is a lot more difficult than it sounds, which is why we learn to communicate with hand and arm signals and other nonverbal messages.

Several studies indicate that the most common employee complaint in businesses today is "lack of communication," with as many as 86 percent of respondents saying poor communication was the source of their workplace failures.

As I have learned the hard way, communicating something

one time is never enough. You must show and tell often. My jury trial coach beat into my head the phrase "repetition is the mother of persuasion." More accurately, repetition is the mother of communication.

It's like the live-fire exercise when the sound of rifle fire fills the air and you can't hear anything anyone says, especially if you are wearing earplugs or your tinnitus kicks in. It doesn't matter that everyone is shouting at the top of their lungs; you can't hear them. You don't know whether the leader wants you to shoot or move because the communication effort fails. Then, once the chaos subsides, the frustrated leader rants about how the team failed to follow commands.

Even when we have functioning radios, star clusters, smoke, chem lights, and other signal-making devices available for communication, in the "fog of war," everything becomes difficult. As military strategist Carl von Clausewitz said, "Everything is very simple in war, but the simplest thing is difficult."[1]

Thus, communication skills must be honed prior to the chaos of a fight. The business world is no different—in times of high stress, messages get muddled. An improper use of a pronoun can cost you a deal; a misplaced comma in a contract can cost millions of dollars. Superior written and verbal communication skills can be the difference between the team executing and failing.

However, even a clear and concise message can fail if it's not repeated often enough. My platoon sergeant used an effective technique to ensure his communication always had maximum range. He said everything three times. And during the most critical information, he would stomp his foot. "Tell 'em what you're going to say, say it, tell 'em what you said, and stomp your foot to give them the answers to the test."

When we can shoot, move, and communicate as a team, we win. However, we never synchronize these individual tasks if we can't do them proficiently. I have found the same to be true in business. I have a peer who runs around with her hair on fire, making sure she's on every social media channel; that she's running ads on TV, radio, and billboards; and that her digital presence includes pay-per-click, over-the-top, and search engine optimization. She's doing everything, but her marketing spend brings her substandard results. Instead of developing competency (and preferably dominance) in a couple of marketing channels, she's diluting her marketing spend and performing poorly at all of them. I've told her multiple times to do what works best, get better at it, and use your resources there. But she insists that she must have a presence on all channels. The problem is that she is not proficient at communicating on any of them.

YES, SIR!

One of the most frustrating parts of running a civilian organization is a breakdown in communication because of differences in philosophy and style. Senior and experienced team members, who may be the best technicians you can hire, may be horrible for organizational growth because they resist change. On the other end of the spectrum, if you hire a bunch of inexperienced people who will say yes to everything, you will lack the safeguard of someone challenging your decisions.

While the highest-ranking leader in any organization owns the role of the visionary responsible for new ideas, that leader must create an environment where diverse thinking occurs on all levels. A team with too many "yes men" loses its identity as a team and takes on the identity of the leader. The commander receives insufficient feedback, and few alternative creative solutions ever arise because of the perils of speaking up. If the team consists of too many "no men," the company loses the value of a leader's vision for the future. It will stagnate and fail to adapt to changing conditions or pivot for growth, and the business will nose-dive into obsolescence.

The team's culture must allow subordinates the freedom and safety to present new ideas, while making space for the wisdom and perspective of more seasoned staff. Great leaders master the art of soliciting criticism to leader-initiated ideas in the boardroom, and alternative ideas that could lead to the result the leader seeks. Often, I find that I am the loudest voice in the room, swaying the team with my conviction rather than logic, reasoning, or data. This can be dangerous because my staff know more about their areas of expertise than I ever will. When no leader challenges my ideas, I grow afraid that I may be failing as a leader, and I remember to ask for feedback.

THE GOOD IDEA FAIRY

On the other end of the spectrum, as a young officer I attended marathon staff meetings run by the "good idea fairy." Any veteran who has served on a staff knows all about the good idea fairy and the consequences of free-flowing communication run amok. In my case, the commander would clearly define the problem and then leave the room for a couple of hours while the staff "worked the problem." Instead of doing as instructed, the staff spewed "good ideas." The commander returned to horrible, half-baked, unrealistic fantasies about how to solve the problem. It was as if once the commander left the room, the brains of the staff left with him and their bodies were occupied by good idea fairies who lacked any knowledge of doctrine, budgets, time constraints, or capabilities. When the commander returned, the staff had prepared a list of all sorts of ideas about new projects on top of the ridiculous solutions to the assigned problem.

Some commanders who lacked a coherent understanding of logistics would invite the good idea fairy to every meeting. Inevitably, someone with a good idea would convince the commander that the idea must be executed, and then another poor soul in the meeting, or not in the meeting, got stuck with the task of making the good idea a reality, even though the idea in no way supported any of the team's priorities.

THE RUSTY EXPERIENCED LEADER

Fortunately, the one personality that kills the good idea fairy is the rusty, crusty old leader who resists change at all costs. This grizzled veteran dislikes any "new ideas." He knows how to do everything because he's been in the army since the Revolutionary War and has seen it all. The crusty old leader shoots down every idea, even the good ones. It's as if he attends meetings for the sole purpose of killing ideas. You can feel his energy when he walks in the room and slowly occupies his seat at the table. He uses his loud breathing when others are talking to let everyone know he disagrees. When that doesn't work, he puts his elbows on the table and buries his face in his hands as if he has a migraine headache or is trying to sleep. When it's his turn to talk, he slowly and confidently explains why the idea will not work, in a condescending tone that makes the entire room feel like he's their third-grade teacher. And while he is obstructionist in nature, he is often correct. His experience carries a lot more weight with the organization than the jumbled thoughts of the good idea fairy. But his rust slows the pace of the organization.

THE PARADOX OF EXCELLENCE AND ACCOMPLISHMENT

So what's better, the resistance of the crusty old leader or the speed and "can do" attitude of the inexperienced person? Probably both. While the experienced person acts as the brakes and the voice of reason, the inexperienced person with initiative can supercharge the project to make it happen—sometimes to the detriment of the organization. Great initiative on the right projects gets fast results, but great initiative on the wrong project can be like running backward: You're not only going in the wrong direction but doing so without visibility of the obstacles ahead. As a leader, it's your job to communicate which of your priorities require perfection and which completion.

Communication often breaks down between the experienced who move with caution and the inexperienced who move with fearless drive. Because they operate at different speeds, at times they appear to speak different languages. I have operated at both levels. Sometimes the sense of urgency we learned in the military takes over and we realize that getting the job done is better than a perfectly performed task. Whenever I know that good is good enough, I hear the first sergeant's voice in my head: "We train to standard, not to time." I have delegated a task to a team member expecting it to be done the same day, only to find a week later that the person is still working on the task. We must communicate when perfection is required and when good is good enough.

Herein lies the communication breakdown. You set a standard of excellence in everything. Not every aspect of a business can sustain consistent excellence in all areas at all times. The natural course of business is that growth breaks systems and people. Sometimes you need a short-term fix to buy time to develop a long-term solution. When you communicate to your team that "nothing less than excellence will do," you have to decide whether you will compromise that standard for the sake of growth and then communicate that priority to the team.

When it comes to delivering a product or service, strive to provide your customers perfection every time. But when it comes to other aspects of the business, we don't have the luxury to perfect every aspect of the business right away. This concept must be communicated cautiously. Perfection cannot be the universal standard, or the standard will grind your organization to a halt. However, you must never communicate that substandard performance is acceptable.

Throughout the years, I have horribly miscommunicated this paradox to my teams. One team member, a former master sergeant, asked me in front of the entire organization, "So do you want it done now or do you want it done right?" Some tasks must be done right, and some must be done now. As a leader, communicating the reality of execution gets tricky. While perfect is the enemy of done, if you accept anything less than perfect, the team will perceive you just lowered the standard of excellence. Communicating a desire to build a rapidly growing, fast-moving team while providing the best service or product on the market may seem like contradictory guidance to your team. Your job as the leader is to simplify the standards and clarify the priorities.

AFTER-ACTION REVIEW

Sustain

1. Set clear standards across the organization.

2. Communicate effectively with repetition, consistency, and redundancy.

3. Recognize when to briefly compromise on excellence to avoid lowering your standards. You can't maintain excellence in everything at all times in a growing organization, but you can maintain clear standards at all times.

Improve

1. Beware of "yes men" and "no men."

2. Losing makes everything harder.

3. Do not allow the "good idea fairy" to run your meetings.

12

HIRE LUCKY GENERALS

To the soldier, luck is merely another word for skill.

—**Patrick MacGill,** *The Amateur Army*

When critics credited Napoleon Bonaparte's wins on the battlefield to luck rather than skill or strategy, he is famously attributed with saying, "I'd rather have lucky generals." Over a century later, General Eisenhower was credited with having the same position: "I'd rather have a lucky general. They win battles." The most successful generals have all been lucky at some point, but they never credit luck. They credit their team, the conditions on the battlefield, the weather, the plan. People who fail, on the other hand, always claim unluckiness. They all blame luck rather than their failure to plan, bad life choices, or poor relationships.

Not all experienced leaders are lucky—lucky generals win. While generals who lose battles and survive do learn lessons, they have not learned the most important lesson, which is how to win a battle. The advice of an unproven "leader" rings hollow. Hire leaders who have "been there, done that," not the unaccomplished leaders who claim they know how to do it but have no victories under their belts. On my first deployment, I, like most of my peers, listened a lot more closely to the leaders who had combat patches on their right sleeves than those who didn't.

We all know the lucky service member in our unit long before his most decisive victory. He wins soldier of the quarter, he never draws charge of quarters (CQ) duty on the weekends, performs well on every test he takes—he seems to luck out with everything. No doubt he works hard, but he also seems luckier than most, and his luck compounds with every accomplishment. We grow sick of the clichés. Luck happens when preparation meets opportunity. The harder you work, the luckier you get. Success and luck seem to go hand in hand.

Now consider the unlucky employee. Always late to work because of traffic, pets, a flat tire, or some life-altering emergency. An untied shoelace caused them to trip and fail the run portion of their physical fitness test. They're financially unstable because they bought a lemon at the used-car lot off post at 19 percent interest. They have the worst luck of anyone you know. Every time they fail because of circumstances beyond their control, the universe conspires against them. Their past results tell the story. For some reason, they always get selected for the worst teams and get suckered into the worst investments. They just can't catch a break.

I recall an unlucky cadet who became a lucky field grade officer and one of the best leaders on my team. Cadet Collins arrived late for an ROTC inspection because of a legitimate flat tire. SFC Stokes, having none of it, blurted out in front of the entire formation, "So what you're saying, Collins, is that you failed to adequately plan and allocate enough travel time to account for contingencies." After a twenty-minute ass chewing in the front-leaning rest position, this cadet learned the following lesson: When we allow ourselves to be victims of circumstance, we forfeit our power to control situations. This is the power of the ownership mindset. If I'm responsible for things that go wrong, I own my future and will ensure they don't happen to me again. If I'm the unlucky victim, I'm powerless to do anything about it.

Cadet Collins learned from this experience, served as a platoon leader in Iraq, a company commander in Afghanistan, and later, as COO at Berry Law, became one of my lucky generals. Lucky generals get results. How did they get lucky? Past performance will tell you how. Evaluate their prior successes. How did they perform in school? While good grades for four years don't guarantee future success, we must attribute classroom performance to something other than luck. Perhaps we cannot narrow it down to intelligence, work ethic, or adaptability, but any of those traits make them appealing candidates. The excellent grades don't tell us the whole story, but they tell us the score.

Similarly, stand-out athletes, leaders of organizations, and top-performing technicians don't achieve without work ethic. In most organizations, the top salesperson is the one who makes the most calls to the best-qualified candidates at the right time. If good luck is the result of hard work, intelligence, adaptability, and a nose for opportunity, "lucky" may be the best qualification for any hire.

Where do you find lucky generals? Well, you won't find them by posting job ads. Lucky generals never need to look for a new position; new positions find them. Perhaps their luck comes from working for the best companies. It's lucky that they have the best reputation, and lucky that they have a record of performance. Senior leaders snatch them up and fight to get them on their leadership team.

For most businesses, identifying lucky generals requires little skill or effort. The difficulty lies in convincing them to join your team. Their abundant luck precludes most lucky generals from ever needing you or your company. They have no shortage of senior officers who want to work with them. Lucky generals are much easier to spot than unlucky employees. Lucky generals are your competitors' best team members—they are well known in their area of expertise, they have massive referral networks and connections, and most importantly they have built a reputation for accomplishing the thing that you need done.

So how do you get the lucky generals to join your team? You start with one. You deliberately seek out the one person you can hire who would increase the value of your company immediately. Often the recruiting process takes a long time. If a lucky general is going to leave a great post to join your team, you will need to educate, seduce, intrigue, and ultimately promise a better opportunity than their current employer. The best players want to go to the best teams, and the best teams constantly recruit the best players. This is why our military's special operations units have such high attrition rates during their qualification programs: They only accept the best. Their high standards attract the best and those who want to be the best. Champions want to play on championship teams with other champions.

As you recruit your lucky generals, consider recruiting three or four at a time. Let all your candidates know you're recruiting the other top talent, and if you can, provide names and future positions of the lucky generals you intend to hire. Best-case scenario, you get all of them. Worst-case scenario, you strike out and get none, but you've sufficiently wooed them. Their closest friends, also lucky generals, will know who you are looking for and that you are building an army led by the best generals.

MOVE UP OR GET OUT

Unlike the military, in the civilian world, you can fire someone without the presumption that you as the leader failed. Some of the worst advice I received in the military came from a battalion sergeant major who told me that soldiers come into the army prequalified. They've passed physical tests, they've scored high enough on the Armed Services Vocational Aptitude Battery (ASVAB), and they made it through basic training. If you can't lead them, it's your fault.

Civilians know this is not true. Every business owner who has done anything worthwhile has hired and fired unlucky employees. There is absolutely no reason to feel shame for a mis-hire. The shame comes from retaining an underperforming employee to the detriment of your team.

The quickest way to destroy a great team is to tolerate consistent substandard performance. As the saying goes, nothing destroys a good employee faster than tolerating a bad one. Hire for specific roles now and the future. If you only hire based on the tasks you need done today, you will outgrow the people you hire. Your lucky generals seek bigger futures. If they don't believe you can provide them bigger opportunities, more money, or more purpose, they will leave your army and join the army that fights bigger battles and slays scarier dragons.

In Ranger School, we had a unique method of eliminating substandard peer performance. At the end of each phase, each student would rank their peers in order of best to worst. The student most often identified as the weakest link could be "peered out" or removed from the class. The team knows who is shouldering more than their share of the task and who is the perpetual underperformer or Blue Falcon. Lucky generals know when they're on a team of high performers and quickly identify low performers.

Over the years we developed a few rules for hiring lucky generals. Only hire people who see a bigger future for themselves and the organization. Never hire someone looking for a slower pace or an easier job. If they're not willing to grow with us, they can't go with us.

In the army officer corps, you can't remain a captain for more than six to eight years before the military kicks you out. If you're not field grade officer material, they won't let you stay in for your twenty years and retire. In most rapidly growing companies, the person who is the top performer today will not remain a top player as the company scales unless that person grows and picks up new skills along the way. This isn't much different than the company commander who must learn to be a field grade officer and a primary staff officer before advancing to become a battalion commander. I knew a lot of amazing company commanders who, once promoted to major, became incompetent staff officers and never got the opportunity to command a battalion.

While some of the big companies in corporate America let a person stay in the same position for twenty-plus years, showing minimal development or improvement along the way, that doesn't work well in rapidly growing small companies. Your top talent today will not be top talent tomorrow. Growing companies must accept that they have not yet hired their best talent. The people you chose to lead your organization three years ago will likely lack the skills and experience you need to grow your team tomorrow. Your most talented technician from two years ago may not have the skills to develop your product or service of the future. As your company grows, that technician may not be willing or able to make the leap.

No person stays with a company forever. Even your best people will voluntarily leave your team. Retirement, burnout, or an opportunity to work for a better company will take some of your best performers.

I know a lot of officers who claim they would have stayed a platoon leader for their entire careers if the army would have let them. It seems like as soon as you become competent at one position, the military moves you to the next position. You repeat this cycle every couple of years. While moving positions and duty stations creates hardships, the movement forces you to grow your leadership skills and knowledge.

The misconception in the civilian world is that once an employee accepts a position, they will want to fill that position for as long as necessary. The sad truth is that people will leave your organization for a better opportunity in a heartbeat. If they can make more money, receive better training, or become part of a more prestigious team, they will leave you no matter how much slack you cut them, how nice you were, or how much they enjoyed your afternoon pizza parties. The best way to keep them is to keep growing your company, which in turn grows their financial options, grows their leadership opportunities, and grows their chances to work with an even better team within your organization.

It's uncomfortable to tell your leadership team and your best talent that you will replace them in a couple of years if they don't grow with the team, but if your team stagnates, you will lose them anyway. It's better to outgrow your best talent than to let your talent go to your competitor and grow with them. Talent loves talent. Thoroughbreds want to run with other thoroughbreds. If the top talent you're recruiting sees you have a stable full of donkeys rather than racehorses, they will not join your team. If your best team members don't seem excited about growth, improvement, and challenges, you've built the wrong team.

Great teams always make room at the top. Your best sales-person may be the primary reason for your growth last year, but if you can hire a better salesperson today, you must. In a perfect world, the two salespeople compete for the top spot and become even better. In the real world, when you hire stars, underperformers get scared, mediocre employees get jealous, and entitled team members feel betrayed.

The company leadership team must serve as a loyal steward of the company. Employees want to feel secure and safe in their work environment, but this is difficult to ensure. You can build stronger, smarter employees by providing outstanding training and maintaining an environment of excellence, but you cannot guarantee the company will be around forever. The best job security is maintaining a high-performing company that grows individual team member capabilities.

In 2001, Jim Collins wrote *Good to Great*, about how some companies made the leap to greatness while others failed.[1] However, almost a third of the "great" companies Collins studied no longer exist. Fannie Mae, the mortgage giant, was famously bailed out by the Treasury during the 2008 market collapse. Circuit City also filed for bankruptcy in 2008. Gillette was purchased by Procter and Gamble in 2005 and faced an $8 billion devaluation in 2019.

In Simon Sinek's book *Leaders Eat Last*, he coined the phrase "circle of safety," which states that since humanity first evolved, we've needed to feel safe within our tribe in order to thrive.[2] The business world is similarly full of conflict and stress, and creating a sense of trust and safety ensures your employees have a solid grounding to perform.

While a great team makes sacrifices for each team member,

safety does not come from slicing a shrinking pie. Safety comes from baking a big enough pie so that everyone can eat enough to feel full. Lucky generals keep their armies well fed. Their hypervigilance and insatiable appetite for victory keep them on the offense.

Think about the bloated companies that play defense. If the company loses market share, they may have to cut jobs, sell to a competitor, declare bankruptcy, or worse, close shop forever. But winning solves all problems: if you continue to grow in your marketplace, you will be safe—even in a bad economy, even if you have to pivot. But growth comes with a sacrifice: you cannot keep mediocre team members forever; you must level up with every hire. In a small company, you can't hire merely to replace someone. If you lose a great team member, you must hire someone better. You have not yet hired your "A Team," and if you erroneously believe you already have, that you'll never hire anyone better than your current team, you as a leader should step down because you are the weak link.

Are you worried that hiring someone better than you will cost you your leadership role? If so, your competitors have already won. Hire everyone better than you. What are you afraid of? Will they take control of the company? Will they expose your incompetence? Will they grow the company further and faster than you? If you don't hire people better than you, your competition will. And if you hire a team that makes you irrelevant to the success of the organization, then you just won the game. The measure of any great military commander is how the organization performs when the commander is away.

Upgrade: Which lucky general will you hire next on your leadership team? You have three choices:

1. Hire in your area of greatest weakness. You may be good at a lot of things, but you'll never be great at everything. There is no such thing as a perfect leader. All leaders have strengths, weaknesses, and areas where they need to improve. If a core functional area of your business lags because of your inexperience or lack of skill, hire someone better than you to fill that role. Just as an individual leader's capabilities do not grow proportionally, team capabilities do not grow proportionally.

   A rapidly growing company can scale quickly with a great sales and marketing team and an average financial arm, until it can't. In the beginning, a strong sales and marketing team will create growth that can be managed by mediocre financial systems by people with mediocre financial abilities, which may be only a bookkeeper or an accountant. But you'll eventually reach a tipping point where you need financial expertise.

   For example, if you can no longer maintain profitability with your great marketing and sales team, you need a strong CFO or controller to ensure that all the money you bring in the front of the business doesn't disappear in the back office.

2. Hire to your biggest pain point or time suck. Yes, as a leader, you must embrace the suck and do the

dirty jobs from time to time, but you should not put yourself in a situation where you have to do them most of the time.

If you lead the organization and you hate your life because of all the HR compliance requirements, it's time to hire that HR director, who happily does the stuff you hate, does it much better than you do, and provides you the freedom to maneuver and do things that actually grow and improve the company.

Conversely, if you like the HR arm of your business, you can stay heavily involved in it and keep doing it until your involvement makes HR the weakest part of the business. At this point, you're back to hiring your greatest area of weakness.

3. Hire for effect. Winners want to be on winning teams. Lucky generals would rather lead a better, smaller army than serve as one of many generals in a large, dysfunctional army. Occasionally you will run across a target of opportunity too good to not engage. Of course, this often happens when you're not ready to hire for that position.

Examples of people we hired even though we were not ready at the time include a highly skilled and accomplished marketing executive from a larger company in our industry who got cut as part of a downsizing initiative; the director of operations of a much larger organization who got passed over for a chief operating officer role, even though she was the COO heir apparent; and a successful entrepreneur who took private equity money and lost control of his company but was willing to join our team to teach us lessons learned about failing the hard way.

Splash! Once we landed these new team members, just like a landing artillery round, our entire organization felt the reverberation and respected us for increasing the organization's firepower and capabilities. These types of hires not only exponentially grow your organizational capabilities; they grow the team's confidence in the leaders who hire the proven lucky generals.

THE STRENGTH TO FIRE

As previously discussed, you have not yet hired your best people, and you will outgrow those who were once your best—if they do not grow at the rate of your organization or faster. You will recognize this before the rest of your team. As you emplace leaders, will they have the strength to help relocate underperformers on their teams to another organization? Former great performers who become underperformers create a lot of emotional baggage for leaders. It takes guts to fire anyone; it takes more guts to fire someone you admire.

The common excuse for not parting ways with an underperformer is that the leader believes they can get the team member "up to standard." But small organizations don't have the luxury of time and cash to train underperformers to get them up to standard; they must use their limited resources to train for excellence. Invest in making the best even better.

But what about no soldier left behind? In combat, we never leave a fallen comrade, but back in garrison, we separate under-performers from the military every day. Even soldiers who performed well during a deployment face military separation for unsatisfactory performance, weight issues, physical fitness failures, or going AWOL.

From time to time, your best team members will have bad luck. If, on balance, they have more bad luck than good luck, they are no longer your best team members. Lucky generals don't win every battle, but they win most of them and they always live to fight another day. Unlucky employees don't fail every time, but they fail enough that it affects the success of the team, and when that happens, they must be retrained or let go. This is the tough part because most people deficient in a skill appreciate training. The unlucky will see the retraining mandate as a personal attack and will resent you for trying to help them. After all, they're not incompetent; they just have "bad luck."

RETENTION AND ATTRITION

In the military, the most popular buzz phrase of senior leaders seemed to be "recruiting and retention." Not only did military recruiters swarm high schools, but every army unit had an assigned "retention NCO" responsible for counseling soldiers about their opportunities to reenlist long before their estimated time in service (ETS) date.

If you want to retain your people, you must invest in their development. The army made endless reenlistment promises to retain soldiers including reenlistment bonuses, specialty schools where soldiers developed specific military skills, paid leave to attend college while on active duty, and sundry programs. The military wisely incentivized their best soldiers to stay.

The goal of any retention program is to retain the high performers and those with potential to become high performers. While an elevated attrition rate can be an indicator of a problem in an organization, it's not always, especially when you are building a championship team. As your organization grows, you will experience periods of high attrition. Greatness comes at the price of not tolerating mediocrity, which means you will raise your standards every year. Most people don't like that, but the right people find inspiration in it.

Think about the attrition rate at basic training and boot camp. About 15 percent of recruits fail out. Approximately 13 to 16 percent of recruits fail to make it through military entrance processing stations (MEPS) every year. Currently the attrition rate at the U.S. Army Ranger School is about 60 percent. Remember that not every soldier gets the opportunity to attend, and most have to earn their slot to the school through an order of merit list.

Similarly, in professional sports, where the best of the best play, the attrition rate is extremely high. The NFL attrition rate per year is 44 percent and rises to 65 percent in the second year.[3] Attrition rates in the NBA (33 percent)[4] and MLB (46 percent)[5] are also high.

However, in your company there is a cost to attrition. The costs of attrition can include lost productivity, decreased morale, headhunting fees, the cost of training new team members to standard, reputational damage, and in some cases, severance pay.

If you are losing team members at an unacceptable rate, you must evaluate four areas of your recruiting and retention.

Recruiting and Hiring Process

Are you hiring highly qualified candidates or are you hiring warm bodies? If you're waiting until you need to hire as opposed to proactively hiring per your growth plan, you will lower your standards and take whoever is available.

You must create and follow a process for weeding out unqualified candidates. If you don't have a process, or a "hiring funnel," you hire unqualified employees. If you want employees who clear obstacles at work, you need to set up obstacles for them to overcome in the hiring process. Think about all the obstacles a recruit must clear before they earn the opportunity to enlist in the military. Some bomb the ASVAB, some fail the physical, and some get flagged during the background check. When you have a great company, you don't just hire anybody, you hire winners who demonstrate a desire to join your team by clearing any and all obstacles in your hiring process. If a prospect balks at your hiring process, how do you think that person will treat your rules and expectations after getting hired?

Great talent rarely comes cheap. But talent has a compounding effect. The more talented people you hire, the more talent you attract. Your investment in hiring quality team members pays dividends in both recruiting and productivity. And when you hire low quality, not only do you pay in terms of reputation, productivity, and team morale, but you pay in progress lost. Few things cost more than a cheap employee. Pay for greatness and demand it in every hire.

Onboarding Process

We all dream of hiring a plug-and-play employee who rushes into the organization and adds value on day one. Perhaps you had a new first sergeant or commander who stormed into your unit and started cleaning it up immediately. This person does not exist in the civilian world.

Even the most experienced professionals need time to understand your culture and the way your team operates before they can improve the organization. The reason military leaders can create what seems like an instant impact is because even though the new commander or first sergeant is new to your specific unit, they have been part of the military culture for years and already know the standards they need to achieve for success.

Outside the military, a ninety-day onboarding process ensures that you set your new team members up for success. This means that not only will you invest in the initial training of new team members, but you will set expectations and standards. Remember the initial counseling sessions when you arrived at your gaining unit? You not only learned expectations but also received specific instructions on how to be a good team member.

Arrive at formation five minutes early, keep the barracks clean, don't go to the banned establishments off post. And then the next day after first formation, you started working with your team.

At your business, some fast-tracking team members may start contributing after a week; others will take the full ninety days. Yes, onboarding is expensive. You pay for ninety days of work with no expectation of work output. Consider the alternative of not onboarding highly motivated people who join your team, only to discover no one is helping them understand their job or the company culture. They lack training, and they have no mentor. No wonder they leave.

Training and Development

Training does not stop after the onboarding process. You need a training calendar, just like the military. Most perishable skills require refresher training at least once a year. I'm not talking about the boring annual death-by-PowerPoint briefs, but actual hands-on training and qualification. Remember weapons systems qualification? We had to qualify annually not only with our assigned weapons but also on any other weapon systems we intended to employ. And, of course, the operating environment changed constantly, which required new training.

As a civilian company, the rate of change outside the organization will require internal changes of systems, software, and processes. All these changes will require training your team to achieve and maintain proficiency. Team members who don't receive adequate training won't perform, and you will either terminate them or they will leave your team out of frustration.

Leadership

If you've developed a competitive hiring funnel, implemented a streamlined onboarding process, and regularly conduct realistic scheduled training, and you are still losing your best employees, it's a leadership problem. If you retain poor leaders, you lose your best team members—it's that simple. Anybody who served in the military knows bad leadership. From credentialed mediocrity (officers who checked every box to become an officer but lack the drive or brains to lead), to competent but toxic leaders, to Blue Falcons, to ghost leaders (otherwise known as quiet quitters, shammers, or oxygen thieves)—you know bad leadership when you see it. Put yourself in the shoes of your team member: if any of these characters served as your first-line leader, would you stay in the organization?

If you hire lucky generals, you won't lose good team members to poor leadership. You will, however, lose low-performing team members and those with fragile egos. Losing those low-performing team members who refuse to meet the standards of the lucky generals builds morale. Good team members never want to leave a great leader. Hire great leaders and your retention problems disappear.

When you hire lucky generals, you commit to building a great organization, but this is only one step on a thousand-mile journey. Once you hire the lucky general, you must retain and develop her. As far as the unlucky team members who have proven they cannot be developed, stop trying. You cannot make them either lucky or happy. Instead, keep your lucky generals happy and they will build your army for you.

AFTER-ACTION REVIEW ═══════════════════════

Sustain

1. Hire proven winners (college athletes, veterans, someone who has achieved something important).

2. Hire the person who has done it, not the person who claims to know how to do it.

3. Hire the person who understands why they won. Those people win again.

Improve

1. Unlucky team members make you unlucky.

2. Losing teaches your people valuable lessons, but losing doesn't teach how to win.

3. Unlucky employees never understand why they failed; they blame luck, they blame others, they blame conditions beyond their control. You cannot fix their fragile egos.

13

HIP-POCKET TRAINING

The art of war teaches us to rely not on the likelihood of the enemy's not coming, but on our own readiness to receive him.

—Sun Tzu, *The Art of War*

"On your feet." I recognized the command but did not expect it. I sat among the half of the platoon that had completed the land navigation course in two of the allotted three hours. Seconds earlier I had ripped open my MRE, hoping to eat and sleep for the next hour while the rest of the platoon finished the course. Boots off, I was letting my feet air out while I ate before changing into dry socks. I saw the soldiers around me scramble to their feet, and I did the same, with bare feet and clean socks in hand.

I identified the sergeant who gave the command as my squad leader, SSG John Hatley. Technically, Sergeant Hatley worked for me, so I didn't have to stand up, but the force of his voice made me react otherwise. SSG Hatley smiled and told us that while we waited for the rest of the platoon, we would be conducting "hip-pocket training." He then explained something more practical than the land navigation course: we would be using our map-reading skills to identify locations for MEDEVAC. MEDEVAC is medical evacuation for injured soldiers, often by helicopter or wheeled vehicle.

SSG Hatley spit out an eight-digit grid coordinate of an imaginary casualty then asked us to provide the eight-digit coordinate of the best landing zone (LZ) for a MEDEVAC helicopter in the area. He used a different area of the map to show other "ideal" LZs and explained exactly what type of terrain pilots needed to land helicopters, which could be loaded with wounded soldiers. He also pointed to an area on the map not accessible by road, which would require helo evacuation.

At the time, my tired body did not want to move, and I struggled to focus. However, the hip-pocket training, which only took fifteen minutes, could be the difference between life and death. Sure, we all knew how to read a topographic map, but the difference between *capable* and *proficient* means a lot of deciding where to land a helicopter to evacuate a wounded soldier. SSG Hatley, a Desert Storm veteran, knew that the fog of war and stress of combat can make simple tasks difficult. By repeatedly training us to locate LZs on a map in a nonstressful environment, he ensured we could perform the task under less-than-optimal conditions, like enemy gunfire.

The "wait" portion of "hurry up and wait," as discussed in the first part of the book, doesn't mean you hang out in the barracks playing video games waiting on the order. Waiting *wastes* time while preparation *saves* time. Staff Sergeant Hatley always said there is never enough time to prepare soldiers for war. Every time we had downtime in the field, he would train us on a new skill. Back then, the repetitive training felt annoying. Today, I understand the impact and am grateful for it. No doubt SSG Hatley's hip-pocket training saved lives over the next two decades of deployments to Iraq and Afghanistan. When I recently discussed the aforementioned example with Hatley, he could not recall that specific training. Perhaps in my mind I associate him with that day because of all the hip-pocket training he conducted for our platoon. In my mind, Hatley is hip-pocket training personified.

I think of it this way: hip-pocket training absorbs the unallocated time in our days that sneak in between the hard hours posted on training schedules. It's the training that we do on the spot, unplanned, with few resources. The term "hip-pocket" training means using whatever is in the immediate vicinity to be your training aid—including whatever you may keep in your hip pocket.

When you have downtime, it's not really downtime—it's training time. In the military, there's no such thing as "spare time." If the first sergeant ever caught you doing nothing, you were going to do one of two things: clean or train. Training was usually the preferred option to sweeping, mopping, and buffing floors; or worse, cleaning the latrine.

First sergeants master hip-pocket training because they must ensure every soldier in the company maintains proficiency in critical skills. First Sergeant Fowler, for example, required his subordinate platoon sergeants to keep hip-pocket training at the ready. You didn't want him to catch your platoon in the barracks or in the field doing anything but eating, sleeping, or training.

For veterans reading this book wondering why the company training schedule posted at your HQ was not sufficient, it comes down to this: the military always wants you to stuff ten pounds of shit into a five-pound bag. Remember your packing list to go to the field or on deployment? You could never get all the gear on the packing list into your rucksack and duffel bags. Same goes for training. You can never be proficient in every military task, even the ones on the training schedule. And of course, proficiency in perishable skills doesn't last unless you continually train and hone those skills.

The publicly published unit training schedule usually provided a well-intended plan, but we all know that as much as the military boasts, "we train to standard, not to time," some training gets pencil whipped so we can move on to the next mission. Hip-pocket training allows us opportunities to train and retrain to proficiency even when the training schedule doesn't allow sufficient time for it.

Of course, there *are* times when waiting means standing around and doing nothing. Standing in formation and senseless mandatory briefings may deprive you of a hip-pocket training opportunity. But when standing around idly *can* be avoided, military leaders seize opportunities to conduct training and prepare soldiers for combat using readily available training aids. When qualifying with our weapons at the rifle range, we set up training stations for assembling and disassembling other weapon systems so that soldiers could train on other tasks while waiting for their turn to qualify. Prior to getting to the firing range, leaders emphasized conducting "washer and dime" drills to improve individual basic rifle marksmanship during any downtime.

The washer and dime drill is an exercise where the soldier practices squeezing the trigger rather than pulling it. The soldier gets in the prone position with his rifle, and his buddy places a small washer or dime on the end of the barrel. The soldier tries to squeeze the trigger so gently that the washer or dime stays on the rifle after dry-firing the weapon. Soon it becomes a game of who can dry-fire ten out of ten times with the dime never falling off the barrel of the rifle. Side note: training can be a lot more fun if you make it a competition.

ALWAYS TRAINING, ALWAYS IMPROVING

The prevalence of hip-pocket training in the military doesn't make it specific to the military. Quick, down-and-dirty, improvised training can be conducted by anyone, anywhere. Whether alone or with a team, un-calendared time becomes a training window, even in civilian life. Don't wait for a platoon sergeant to come along and force training on you. Be proactive, know your deficiencies, study ways to improve, and develop the habit of conducting hip-pocket training whenever you feel unproductive, bored, or stuck.

At its core, hip-pocket training combines time management and skill mastery. If you have time and know you need to train on a specific skill, then use that time to train on that skill. It's that simple.

Most people squander "spare time" on their smartphones, scrolling through multiple social media channels, shopping online, surfing the internet, or playing video games. We all have the same twenty-four hours in a day. It's how you use your time that matters. I have yet to meet the person who truly does not have the time to take the necessary actions to achieve their most important goal. Lack of discipline, focus, and desire kills goals, not lack of time. President Barack Obama made time to run every day. If the commander-in-chief had time to exercise every day, so do you.

Deep down, we all know our strengths and weaknesses and what must improve to achieve the results we desire. Advancing to our next achievement requires education, training, and development. Hip-pocket training is rarely physically demanding or resource intensive—those types of activities should already be on your calendar as scheduled training.

We manage grueling schedules, making it difficult for us to train and study the subjects we need to learn to become proficient or, better yet, experts. "Leaders are readers," and the easiest hip-pocket training requires nothing more than picking up a book and holding it to your face. Don't have time for that? Audiobooks allow us to absorb that information while waiting in traffic, in line at the supermarket, and even while exercising. It's amazing how much mental training we accomplish when we make listening to audiobooks or reading a habit.

Hip-pocket training can also include acting as the platoon sergeant in someone else's life. If you see team members struggling in an area where you excel, offer to train them. Not only will you improve the lives of the people you help, but you will keep your skills sharp while boosting your morale and theirs. More importantly, when you pick the right people, you find training partners who will return the favor and hold you accountable.

Bring your idea of hip-pocket training into your organization. I am always on the lookout for an opportunity to train. I carry a list with me that consists of areas where we can improve. Training opportunities disguised as delays show up every week. Sometimes the training on my list can be done in as little as five minutes per week. In the five minutes of downtime I could have spent checking my email for the twentieth time today, I trained my team on a small but important skill.

Bosnia range fire training

THE TRAINING HABIT

It's easy to fall into bad habits after separating from the military. You spent years waking up at five in the morning, exercising regularly, learning intensively, and training to proficiency. Then someone hands you a DD214 and magically it all stops.

Nobody in the civilian world trains like the military. If I could do it, I would run a boot-camp-style immersion plan for the first ninety days for all new team members. We'd start with physical training in the morning, conduct real-world training all day, study hall at night, and have all meals provided at a world-class dining facility with healthy options. Pure focus and discipline with team building—all like the immersive training we experienced in the military. As the saying goes, "The U.S. Army does more by 7:00 a.m. than most people do all day."

Compare the early morning activity in your company to the early morning activity on a military base. On a military base, by 6:30 a.m. nearly everyone on base conducts physical training or has started the workday. No occupied beds exist in any barracks across the base.

Training habits within the confines of a military installation become a training lifestyle. Training in the field differs from training in garrison, but the disciplined focus toward proficiency remains the same. Shared energy for excellence and a sense of purpose enhance training.

After the military, I've seen too many veterans fall into lazy behaviors, avoid training, and allow skills to perish. To overcome this, training must become part of your lifestyle again.

First, identify the skills you want to develop. For some, this means listing the skills they need to develop to become world-class in their chosen field. For others, this means "checking the box" of getting a degree or certification.

Next, plan for the training on your list. Every week, look at your list and block time for specific training events on your calendar. In Chapter 6, we discuss creating a calendar based on priorities. For some leaders, training is a daily calendared priority. Anticipate lulls in your day, and commit to fill them with the training you need. If you don't plan the training, time vampires will suck up the unplanned time on your calendar and you will never achieve your goals. But, if you have your hip-pocket training ready, and you habitually train in your time off, you will naturally think about hip-pocket training as soon as you find yourself in a lull.

Outside of a military environment, calendared training usually takes a back seat to deadlines, meetings, and emergencies. However, when deadlines get postponed and meetings get canceled, white space appears on your calendar. Usually that white space appears after it is too late to schedule anything significant. This is the perfect time for hip-pocket training. The same calendar tasks that took priority over your training are gone, and now, if you are prepared, you have time to train.

Hip-pocket training is your contingency plan, it's your excuse-proof plan, and it's your plan when you don't have a plan. When you constantly train and prepare for a bigger future, you develop a hypersensitivity to opportunities. Once you condition your brain to look for training opportunities, you will see them everywhere.

Cultivate focus. Plan ahead. Whether you carry a briefcase,

a purse, or a rucksack, plan for those moments when opportunities to conduct hip-pocket training present themselves. Find material that will make you a better person, professional, or parent—whatever area in life you want to excel in. Your training aids will not magically appear when you need them. If you want to be a great trial lawyer, you must master the rules of evidence. Carry a copy of the rules of evidence with you and make a habit of breaking the book out during any downtime. If you want to learn business strategy but don't have time to go back to school just yet, develop a reading list and get audiobooks that you listen to every time you get into your car. The point is to keep your goal top of mind and bask in the satisfaction that you are taking steps toward that goal no matter how small.

You only live one life. You only have one opportunity to become the person you want to be. You won't become that person unless you deliberately and relentlessly train to become that person. Unlike the military, the only person who can publish a training schedule to get you to your destination is you. If you truly want to make the best of your situation, focus time and energy on becoming proficient in the skills in which you need to excel to achieve your goals. Always have your training aids/ materials at the ready, even when there appears to be no space for training on your calendar that day.

Athletes do this intuitively. Soccer players waiting for the next game will start juggling, dribbling, and practicing shooting. Sprinters stretch and do plyometric exercises between races. When the great athletes appear to be sitting still, they are busy visualizing their perfect performance.

While training acquires skill, growth requires development. Great military officers do not become great through training alone. For example, reading helps leaders broaden their thoughts. But reading every book on military strategy, although a great first step, does not make a great officer. Reading all rules of evidence doesn't help a trial lawyer who never puts them to use in the courtroom. Reading books on football won't make you a star running back. Business school lectures won't provide the full benefit until you actually apply them.

We've all seen the shadow boxer at the gym, the kid shooting hoops on a deserted basketball court, the orator practicing a speech in an empty auditorium, the musician performing in the empty music hall. They train incessantly; they get their reps in with or without a coach. They have mastered hip-pocket training, but without a mentor to guide and develop them, they will never reach their potential. No one achieves greatness alone.

Growing teams of leaders requires both training and development. While a person can train alone, development requires another person—a coach or mentor. As I write this book, Berry Law is in the planning process of building its own courtroom to train and develop other lawyers. Great athletes seek locations that provide realistic training and coaches who can develop them to become next-level players. As leaders we provide our teams realistic training opportunities and coach our teams to develop even greater skills. This not only retains talent in our organization but also attracts outside talent.

The best organizations never stop training. They know that their team is either getting better every day or getting worse;

they know the same is true for their competitors. However, we can't focus solely on improving today's skills and tasks; we must also train for the skills we need to develop in the future.

Whenever we hit plateaus and our business stops growing, it's usually because we became so focused on the execution of daily tasks that we neglected the improvements and skills that we needed to develop to facilitate the next stage of growth. What got you here won't get you there. You must have a future-focused mindset, which requires perpetual improvement of your current skills while also developing skills needed in the future.

While training increases employee satisfaction and retention, training for skills necessary for the next stage of growth shows the team a commitment to growing a bigger future for the organization. No amount of impressive presentations about a leader's vision will have the impact of a leader's investment in developing future capabilities in the organization. Great team members appreciate a leader's investment in their individual professional development for next-level growth. The leader's actions show a commitment not only to growing the organization but to growing its people so that they can experience a bigger future as the company moves to the next level. Team members don't fear they will be left behind during the next phase of growth, because the leader has committed to preparing them for it by arming them with the training necessary to succeed in even greater roles.

By training the team for the future, you as the leader prove your commitment to the vision and the team. Team members buy into the vision because your actions make the vision real to them. They can see it in the perpetual training for the future.

If you want to be the best, you will never let a training opportunity pass. Every missed opportunity breeds entropy. Your enemies and competitors will see your progress, and they will either hate you for it or outwork you—if you let them. Training for the future organization you wish to become is imperative. Incorporating training into your daily routine may be the small but necessary habit that will push you to your full potential.

AFTER-ACTION REVIEW

Sustain

1. Training must be a part of your culture.

2. Training must be calendared, but it must also be a habit.

3. Training must be realistic.

Improve

1. Not all training needs to be planned. Hip-pocket training provides spontaneous training opportunities.

2. Training can be done alone. Development requires a coach or mentor.

3. Train now for skills and competencies that your team will need in the future.

Part III
DOMINATE

14

CADENCE

We are stronger together than we are alone.

—Attributed to Walter Payton

Repetitive execution establishes a rhythm. The battle rhythm, the flywheel, and the interconnected efforts of the organization must be synchronized.

Remember those mornings where you ran in formation? In unison? When you ran at the pace of your platoon sergeant's cadence, shouting loud—and sometimes offensive—cadences? Some soldiers would want to pick up the pace, but they knew others who fell to the back would never be able to keep up. Those in peak physical condition would travel to the back of the formation to the struggling teammates and help them. Push them. Get them to ignore the pain and drive on. We didn't let team members fall out.

What happened over time? After habitually doing PT in the morning over and over, results became visible. That person who struggled at the back of the formation made their way to the middle of the pack, or maybe even to the front to control the pace for the other soldiers. They put in the effort and found themselves rewarded for doing so. In the end, with the help of their fellow soldiers and by making PT a habit, those who struggled became stronger. And those who continued to struggle and showed no progress quit.

Would that struggling soldier have pushed through those hardships on their own? If they hadn't joined the military and been taught to push through the pain and to form strong habits, would they have made the same positive improvements?

Exercising in cadence allows an entire unit to feel a sense of collaborative accomplishment. It builds relationships and allows the strongest on your team to show their leadership abilities. Those of us who excel in PT don't like running at the same pace as slower team members. However, leaders must learn to run stride for stride with those still working on increasing their endurance, unless they are running with a pack of gazelles.

At the Infantry Officer's Basic Course, the NCOs broke all the 2LTs into three groups for morning PT: the fast group, the medium group, and the slow group. Anyone who ran a sub-twelve-minute two miles, or wanted to, joined the fast group. The medium group invited the fourteen-minute two milers. The slow group invited those who barely passed the Army Physical Fitness Test (APFT). I joined the fast group.

My pride from joining the fast group came from the previous year of training where I reduced my two-mile time by over three minutes and dropped twenty pounds. During my unimpressive college football career, which consisted of two years of riding the bench, I judged my fitness based on strength, muscle mass, quickness, and sprinting speed. I spent a year changing my body to become a distance runner who could max the APFT by running a sub-11:54 two-mile run.

I took an enormous amount of pride in running in the fast group every morning. I earned the right to be in the top group. Even though there were guys in the fast group who had run sub-ten-minute two-mile times, I ran in the same formation as them, shouting out the same cadences. Sure, I thought I would die as our formation passed the airfield and we headed up Cardiac Hill, but it was worth it. I never fell out of a run. I also never felt better after a run, once I started breathing again.

Cadence is all about working together and igniting a sense of urgency under those who may otherwise not keep pace. When it comes to running in formation and sounding off in cadence, the biggest fear everyone has is falling out. Nobody wants to be the weakest member of the unit. The same applies to your civilian life and your professional career. There is a certain amount of understanding inside a business that the group cannot move forward as a unit unless everyone maintains the same cadence. If team members fail to sound off, keep pace, or stay in step, the entire organization suffers.

YOU CAN ONLY GO AS FAST AS THE SLOWEST TEAM (MEMBER)

The greatest and worst thing about running in cadence is that you can only go as fast as your slowest team member. Nothing tests an organization's unity and teamwork like a physical challenge. Individually you may repeatedly max your physical fitness test, but if the rest of your team struggles to pass, your perfect score won't matter much when you finish as a team.

Everybody must sound off when you have a cadence. Everybody runs and everybody is in step. We all take our first step with our left leg, and as we run, we all feel the same foot strike the ground at exactly the same time. If one person gets out of step, it throws the entire run out of rhythm. That's all it takes. One person. And then we trip all over each other.

Of course, in the military, we learn to march in cadence before we run in cadence. For new military recruits, marching (a.k.a. walking) in formation is a difficult task. Drill sergeants take a gaggle of new recruits and work for weeks to get them to march in step with arm swings nine inches to the front and six inches to the rear. After everybody learns to march in step, following cadence, the drill sergeants add complexity by incorporating turning and flanking movements. Now the team moves in unison like a machine and maneuvers flawlessly on command.

This daily cadence at Berry Law has become paramount to our success. Our organization cannot move forward in sync if one section of the team is not aligned. So it is my job as a leader to keep every section in rhythm so that we can maneuver as an organization.

When one section moves faster than the others, we trip all over ourselves. If our team can't move at full speed because we failed in our hiring forecast to hire enough lawyers and paralegals, our marketing team must slow down their tempo and cut spending to reduce the number of leads to our intake team. Our intake team can't help potential clients at a normal pace because legal operations are at capacity. Our facilities manager must do what she can to reduce the cost of the empty space we leased for the new hires that we never hired, and the finance team now must forecast and recalculate based on our lower-than-expected headcount.

So how do we make sure we don't fall out of step, out of sync, or out of cadence?

For starters, we speak a common language that everyone understands throughout the organization by calling out cadence loud and clear.

One example is our "stand to" meetings, which we have every Monday morning. The name stems from Rogers' Rangers and the idea that we are at the ready—ready to stand. It's the time for us to prepare ourselves for the week so that we can all move through it together, in step, shoulder to shoulder. Nobody is thrown off guard by a different cadence. Everything is planned, and we are ready to attack the week before it attacks us. By 0815 every Monday morning, we know our plan for the week.

At the end of every week, we conduct a weekly "all call" in which we celebrate our victories as a team and announce individual wins. All call takes place on Friday afternoons at 4:45. At this point, our weeklong sprint in formation is over. Nobody has fallen out of formation; the cadence has allowed us all to move forward together. And now we celebrate the victories we have earned during the week because of this preparedness. With loud music, large screens, and the team gathered with drinks in hand, we celebrate not only the biggest wins of the week but our progress toward our three annual goals. We also recognize personal achievements from the week.

Excellent results also come when activities inside of an organization maintain synchronization. Cohesiveness has allowed us to work on big appeals and large trials where multiple people within our organization serve different functions to achieve a common goal. Our results come quickly when we work together in alignment and unison, remaining in cadence the entire way to achieve winning results.

DON'T GET OUT OF STEP

Doing things in unison can be frustrating at times. At my first duty station I loathed the days when we ran in formation during "morale runs" because I wasn't able to push myself. Running a ten-minute mile at an airborne shuffle pace didn't invigorate me. Running at the same speed as the old general officer who ran out in front of the unit with his flags waving wasn't what I would call a workout. And of course, the accordion effect cannot be prevented when running in formation. You always experience the straining force that slows you down to a walk while you wait for others to catch up followed by the sprinting to catch up to the group in front of you.

But at the much smaller infantry company level, there is something special about running in formation. Sounding off comical cadences allowed everyone to forget about their sore bodies and simply run—focusing on the cadence rather than the pain and the fatigue. Sometimes the cadences were downright dirty. Other times they were inspiring. The fluctuation allowed runs to remain fresh. And there were always those who loved to lead the cadence with strong, motivating voices. There is something infectious about the soldier who can sing at the top of his lungs and bellow out a powerful cadence when the fatigued team gasps for air.

The most important thing about cadences is sounding off together. We all shout those words while pushing our bodies in step. Cadences keep us unified and moving in the same direction, at the same speed. Cadences tell us we're a team and remind us we will leave no soldier behind. We fight together and we finish together.

Cadences face more resistance in the civilian world. Too many coworkers take single-minded approaches to growth. They worry about propelling themselves further up the corporate ladder, but they fail to realize that a company is only as great as its weakest link. Silos emerge outside of the company's cadence, causing disruption. Teams and individuals move at a pace detached from the organization, hoarding information, disregarding SOPs, and implementing different operating systems. The once well-oiled machine breaks down and the company stops growing.

As a veteran, you bring the wisdom of cadence into the lives of civilians. The team must follow a cadence to overcome the challenges of rapid growth. The cadence will keep the team together during periods of chaotic growth.

Even strong leaders get out of sync and alignment with the rest of the team from time to time. When this happens, the leader must adjust the operational tempo of the organization. It's not uncommon for the marketing team, at the leader's urging, to step on the gas and capitalize on opportunities while the finance team urges caution. Sometimes the finance team is right. Other times finance is the weakest link. Ultimately what matters is that the leader stays in sync with the organization and the teams stay in sync with each other. The leader must maintain awareness of all moving parts of the organization and ensure they move in harmonious cadence, even when they disagree.

Your company's battle rhythm is not classified information. Every team member must know when team meetings occur. The team meetings occur the same time each day, week, month, quarter, or whatever frequency is necessary, and you ensure all meetings are calendared and the appropriate leaders receive invites and reminders.

For example, our leadership team meets every Tuesday at 11:00 a.m. for sixty minutes. The agenda is always the same, and the issues are listed and distributed prior to the meeting. By the end of the meeting, all issues are resolved, tabled, or killed. What happens if a leader cannot make the meeting? We have the meeting. We don't reschedule, we don't cancel, and we don't start late. Meetings start on time, follow the agenda, and end on time regardless of who is present, just like in the military.

Our leadership team also meets quarterly to make sure we are on track to meet our one- and three-year goals. The quarterly meetings last an entire day. They begin at 0800 and end at 1700. The subordinate teams have their battle rhythm aligned with the leadership team's battle rhythm to facilitate the dissemination of critical information in a timely manner.

Do we have emergency meetings? Yes, but those are infrequent because we have a rhythm designed to reduce disruptions to allow our team to stay highly productive and in cadence. If we allow a lot of unplanned meetings, we absolutely kill our cadence and our productivity. For this reason, we adhere to the following rule: if a problem can be resolved without a meeting, no meeting.

The real magic in a cadence is efficiency. When we all move at the same speed, we stop chasing our tail, we move unified in one direction, at one speed, toward one destination. The cadence is merely the vehicle to advance toward our shared objectives.

Cadence builds a scalable culture, and a scalable culture primes an organization for growth. An aligned organization can grow because its efforts become synchronized. Of course, the bigger you grow, the harder it is to stay in cadence. Without a cadence, the team suffers from bottlenecks and the team trips all over itself. You can only go as fast as your bottleneck allows, so put your slow runners up front and figure out how to make them faster, right? Well, cadence doesn't solve bottlenecks in a fractured culture.

In 2005, Sprint acquired Nextel Communications, making the merged company the third-largest telecommunications company in the U.S. Sprint hoped to grow each company's consumer base by cross-pollinating with the other. Soon after the merger, however, a swath of Nextel's executives and managers exited the company. Why? Sprint maintained its bureaucratic nature and substandard customer service reputation, while Nextel sought to cling to its entrepreneurial roots, focusing on customers' needs and desires. The two companies maintained two separate headquarters, with Sprint's executives maintaining all approval authority, leaving Nextel frustrated and out of the loop. Sprint's stock price suffered, and in 2008, the company wrote off an astonishing $30 billion loss. The companies simply could not move at the same speed in cadence.

Ultimately, cadence is about culture. Large, bureaucratic companies move slowly, while smaller, entrepreneurial companies move fast. Fast-moving teams rarely find cadence with slow-moving bureaucracies. Fast runners hate to run slow, even while running in formation. Mergers and collaborations can be powerful opportunities so long as all stakeholders can agree on a mutual cadence.

AFTER-ACTION REVIEW

Sustain

1. Cadence maintains organizational alignment.

2. At the organizational level, major efforts must be synchronized.

3. Cadence builds culture.

Improve

1. If you get out of step, the entire organization stumbles.

2. Keep your slow runners in the front; their speed is
    your constraint. You can only grow as fast as your
    slowest developing capability.

3. The bigger you get, the harder it is to stay in cadence.

15

FEEDBACK IS A GIFT

There is no failure. Only feedback.

—Attributed to Robert Allen

As veterans, we surround ourselves with people who, for the most part, recognize strong leaders. We learn leadership skills from those who have led others in combat and in life, and we pass those skills down to others.

Ironically, the more we develop as leaders, the more we learn that no leadership rules or principles can be absolute. As a lieutenant I got burned from time to time for taking responsibility for the failure of my cohort. I hated to be called out for a failure and then redirect fire on a peer. When something went wrong, I apologized, without explanation, and took responsibility in front of the chain of command.

I remember one particular rotation at the National Training Center (NTC) where several lieutenants, including myself, were charged with creating overlays for the battle maps, which would be on the tactical operating center (TOC) walls during the training exercise. The operations officer assigned each lieutenant an overlay except the least competent lieutenant, whom we'll call "Nick."

Knowing my handwriting appears sloppy on acetate, and that I lack skill in drawing graphics, I accepted Nick's offer for assistance. Nick worked on the bottom of the overlay—the graphics portion—while I worked on the top. When all the lieutenants had completed their projects, the operations officer stopped in to inspect our work. He spot-checked every overlay. When he got to my overlay, he looked only at the portion I completed and told me it was ugly but good enough.

An hour later, I could hear the battalion commander yelling at the operations officer about some of the graphics. The operations officer called me into the briefing room and told me to fix the graphic on the spot. At that point, I didn't know which was worse, the fact that I had not inspected Nick's work on the graphics or that I had let him work on the project. Sure, I could have blamed Nick. It was, after all, his fault. We also held the same rank—had I dimed him out, I would not have been blaming a subordinate, I would have been blaming a peer with my same experience level and pay grade.

A few weeks later, at the culmination of the exercise, the senior leadership conducted the AAR. When the brigade commander noticed the peer critiques seemed watered down, I regretted not alerting Nick to the mistake he made on the graphics. As discussed earlier in the book, "a dime dropped is a dime well spent." We must call out our peers and buddies when they fail to meet our expectations. Holding back criticism selfishly deprives your subordinates, peers, and bosses of the opportunity to improve. As a leader you can't withhold information, insights, and opportunities for improvement because you don't want to hurt feelings. I say "selfish," because if you are holding back because you fear conflict or embarrassing someone, that's your own struggle. You may want to humbly deliver the information so that your team member does not see it as a personal attack, but as a leader you cannot withhold that information.

It seemed during every AAR, at least one military leader would try to explain deficiencies in their actions and make excuses rather than graciously accept the feedback and discuss how to fix the problem in the future. All we can do as leaders is give the feedback. How individuals react to that feedback says a lot more about their maturity and mental stability than our delivery of the critical information.

While big egos among military officers abound, they do not overshadow the egos of civilian professionals. At our firm, one of our team members was married to a man we'll call "Rob," who, after experiencing great professional success in business, decided to go to law school. Over the years I saw Rob at law firm events and received updates on his budding new career. Rob worked for a large firm with consummate professionals who treated him with collegiality and respect. Rob boasted about his firm's mentoring program and that even the critiques were "nice" and "constructive." Rob's termination from that firm surprised him. He could not understand how the firm could fire him when he "did everything right." I confronted one of my friends who was a partner at the big firm about this "injustice."

My friend gave a much different version of the events. The big firm provided Rob frequent feedback regarding substandard performance. Apparently, this team liked to use the compliment sandwich method where they would tell him what he was doing well, followed by where he needed to improve, followed by another compliment. All Rob heard were the compliments. The leader kept explaining that the firm needed to do a better job getting him up to speed, so Rob assumed the firm believed that the firm bore responsibility for his substandard performance. Thus, Rob's termination shocked him and his family.

I don't particularly enjoy listening to the self-reflection of team members. However, every time I give feedback, I do not let the employee leave the counseling session until they answer this question: "What did you just hear me tell you?" Most of the time, the brief-back affirms that the team member understands the message I am sending. However, sometimes either the person will see the feedback as a harsh personal attack, or worse, they will think you are apologizing because you as a leader are responsible for their failure.

Brutal honesty doesn't have to be brutal. You can be honest without being offensive. Whenever I can use objective data in my feedback, it reduces sensitivity to that feedback. The difference between "you're failing" and "for the last two weeks your numbers have been 70 percent off target" are conceptually very similar, but one is a subjective assignment while the other is an objective fact.

The potential for employees to react negatively to constructive feedback discourages many leaders from giving it, when in truth, team members want to know where they stand. Find ways to give it without destroying the relationship.

YOU'RE NOT RESPONSIBLE FOR EVERYTHING

One of the biggest misconceptions I developed as a civilian small business leader came from my military experience: that the leader must accept responsibility for everything. For years, if something went wrong, I took responsibility. Can't pay overhead this month? My fault, I didn't enforce attorney billing standards. The SEO vendor failed to coordinate with the website designer? My fault, I failed to supervise their coordination. No more coffee in the break room? My fault, I should have given the office manager better direction. Client didn't pay his bill? My fault, I didn't do a good enough job explaining the written fee agreement to her. Regardless of whether the root of the problem uncovered an unproductive employee, an incompetent vendor, or an act of God, I claimed responsibility.

The problem I created by taking responsibility for everything was that the team started to believe I bore responsibility for everything, which eroded their sense of personal responsibility. "Don't worry, it's John's fault, and he will take care of it." I had killed initiative in the organization. By claiming all the responsibility for our failures, I failed to hold the team accountable. I was again letting the least competent lieutenant (Nick) screw up my projects and publicly taking the blame. Somehow, I forgot that "a dime dropped is a dime well spent." And my amnesia on this point slowly strangled the organization with chokepoints, inefficiencies, and complacency.

I filled my days solving problems that I should have delegated. I felt like a goalie on a soccer team. I spent a lot of time anticipating shots and the rest of my time blocking shots. Some days I solved the problem that never was; other days I could feel, see, and hear the problem coming at me at a hundred miles an hour. Like a goalie, I played defense, which prevented me from playing offense. I focused on keeping the organization alive rather than growing it. Unlike a goalie, I had no net behind me. It felt more like a cliff. If my defense wasn't good enough, the ball would go over the cliff and drag our entire organization with it.

One day in an emergency meeting about staffing a large project, I sensed a lack of engagement and effort. The team appeared to search for answers on their laptops and smartphones, but no one volunteered solutions. I left to take a phone call. When I returned ten minutes later, I observed the team talking—but not about the staffing problem. I asked the senior team member, "What's the purpose of this meeting?" The senior team member provided a satisfactory response showing she understood the scope and importance of the problem. I said, "Good, now solve it." When I came to work the next morning, the team presented a solution. From that moment forth, I pushed most of the problems to the senior team member who felt like she finally had received permission to lead.

RESPONSIBILITY TO GIVE FEEDBACK AND RECEIVE IT

Some of the greatest lessons I learned about feedback came from leaders who failed to seek it or give it.

When I decided to leave active duty to pursue law school, I submitted paperwork at division HQ so that I could transfer to the National Guard and receive tuition assistance. When I exited the front door of division, transfer paperwork in hand and eyes on my folder, I almost bumped into the chest of my battalion commander. The BN CDR looked stunned, angry, and slightly scared, and rightfully so. Infantry lieutenants do not go to division HQ for no significant reason.

"What are you doing here at division, Berry?" he barked. I stammered, "Sir, I intended to tell you during my annual OER counseling last month, but it never happened. . . . I mean, we never had a meeting, so um . . . I have a deadline to submit my paperwork to transfer to the National Guard to go to law school."

Perhaps in that moment the BN CDR thought that if he would have conducted my scheduled annual senior rater counseling the previous month, I would have stayed in the army. Of course, it would not have made a difference in my plans. But he would have learned I was leaving, which may have helped him to plan to replace me and the six other lieutenants who left the battalion that summer to pursue civilian careers.

Like most lieutenants, I dreaded writing my officer evaluation support form, and I lacked interest in reviewing my performance with my boss's boss. While I cared deeply about my soldiers' opinions of me, I barely thought about the impressions I made on my commanders. Part of the reason for my apathy toward senior leader feedback came from my intent to never become a career military officer. A top block or center of mass rating from my senior rater made no difference in my future plans.

Of course, when I wrote OERs (Officer Evaluation Reports) and NCOERs for my leaders, I understood the impact of the annual evaluation on their careers. I perceived most of my NCOs planned to serve for twenty years or more to earn military retirement. I wanted to ensure that I helped all my subordinate leaders achieve their goals. I tried to provide feedback frequently enough that their annual evaluations contained no surprises. They took their careers seriously, and I took their careers seriously too.

The NCOER/OER *requirement* to provide feedback on both performance and potential made the tool highly valuable. I found that feedback on past performance resonated more when I explained how it influences perceptions about potential for promotion.

In hindsight, the military evaluation system worked much better than I perceived at the time. A one-page evaluation filled out front and back seems light compared to the fluff-filled evaluations I see HR companies offering today.

Recently, our HR director sent me a proposed eight-page annual employee evaluation provided by a consultant. I noticed the evaluation provided plenty of room for opinions, subjective ratings, and explanations but not much emphasis on rankings and factual justifications or metrics. Furthermore, the proposed employee evaluation lacked safeguards against rating inflation. In fact, had I used the proposed evaluation, every single person in the company could have had a perfect score. All 125 of our employees could legitimately claim they were the best because the "evaluation" allowed for it.

Compare this modern HR foolishness with the army's OER/NCOER system. First, blanket statements unsupported by facts don't get officers top-block ratings. Similarly, NCOs don't get "excellent" ratings without a factual justification. This means the evaluations are based on what you actually did during the rating period, rather than the subjective feelings your boss has about you, your performance, and your potential.

In the military, HR (the S1 or G1) ensures that we validate any assertions made in evaluations with facts and numbers, especially for top performers. Often the S1 would kick back evaluations because comments were not quantified by any historical data or facts.

For example, one commander may write, "1LT Smith is the best platoon leader in the battalion. He excels in PT, leadership, and tactical knowledge." That commander could even rate that lieutenant "above center mass," which is reserved for the top 25 percent. However, that OER would get kicked back because the rating is not factually substantiated.

A better commander would write, "1LT Smith consistently scores a perfect 300 on the APFT. His platoon maintains the highest APFT average in the battalion with an average score of 290. 1LT Smith also obtained the highest score of any officer in the BN during Table XIII Gunnery. During the Brigade NTC rotation this year, 1LT Smith's platoon killed ten enemy tanks, twice as many as any other platoon in the brigade. 1LT Smith is in the top 1 percent of the three hundred lieutenants I have worked with in my sixteen-year career."

And what would happen if the battalion commander tried to rate over 25 percent of his lieutenants "above center mass"? The battalion commander's senior rater profile would get crushed and all the lieutenants he rated "above center mass" would receive a "center mass" rating on their permanent OERs. In other words, if a senior rater tried to game the system and rate all his leaders at the top, none of them would be at the top after the ratings were validated by higher headquarters.

It seems businesses today like to use annual evaluations as coaching tools rather than to objectively rate leaders based on their performance over the past year and their potential for promotion. In the military, the evaluations would not only discuss performance and potential but also provide recommendations to senior leadership such as "promote ahead of peers" or "promote with peers." The only downside was that a negative OER also required a lot of justification. You had to sufficiently document why a dirtbag did not meet standards. The "referred OER" gave the poorly performing officer the opportunity to appeal a less-than-average annual evaluation report. Based on the effort required to substantiate a *referred* OER, commanders were reluctant to accurately document poor performance in annual performance reports.

What about the coaching tools? They have their use, but they are separate from an evaluation report. The army's coaching tool is the OER support form (OERSF). Officers list their goals and aspirations for the upcoming year after reviewing the aspirations of their commanders two levels up the chain of command. This allows the officer to align her goals with the organization's objectives.

At Berry Law, we communicate with absolute transparency about how team members performed for the year. Our team members receive weekly scorecards that list their KPIs, but in the annual review we get even deeper into their data to help them not only understand their performance but also understand what actions may be helping or hurting their efforts to achieve their goals.

The evaluations need to be results-based. When evaluating a leader, I answer these questions:

1. How did the leader's team perform based on team metrics
   a. compared to internal standards?
   b. compared to other teams?

2. How did the leader's individual team members perform
   a. compared to internal standards?
   b. compared to peers?

3. What were their major objectives for the quarter, and did they accomplish them?

4. What big wins did they have that set the example for their team?

5. What big wins did their subordinates achieve?

Note: Coaching tools serve a separate purpose than a performance evaluation. A performance evaluation is a report card of past performance. A coaching tool uses past performance feedback to create a future plan for improvement.

THE GIFT OF FEEDBACK

Whether we received feedback from an annual performance evaluation, a word of caution from an observer controller during a field exercise, a challenge from a mentor, a jab from a subordinate during an after-action review, or a bad score on a command climate survey, we treated feedback as a gift in the military.

Leaders often boast that they make "data-driven" decisions. We expect our leaders to test and measure their hypotheses and make objective and sound decisions. Measuring and coaching team members to perform is no different.

In sports, it's easy. We measure the performance of runners, swimmers, and cyclists based on their event times. If the times improve, the training is working. If times don't improve, we adjust the training. In other sports, we consider data points and other statistics. Teams grade players on assists, batting average, on-base percentage, rushing yards, interceptions, and so forth. Even after a team wins a game, the coaches and athletes go back into the stats to find ways to improve. Their competitive nature drives them to seek out the data about their performance and the performance of their competitors.

You want competitive people on your team, and competitive people need to know whether they are winning or losing every day. Salespeople in every organization get their numbers daily, but shouldn't everybody have the same opportunity for feedback? A lot of business coaching programs tell us everybody must have at least one number that they strive to achieve every day. A more effective organization provides team members with multiple metrics, but not too many. We have found that the optimal number in our organization is three to five. When we focus on only one metric, we often default to revenue, which fails to provide a holistic picture of performance. When we list over five metrics, team members can get overwhelmed.

Think back to school. Everyone received a report card with grades for several disciplines. Some classes had daily quizzes. Other classes only provided grades after a couple major projects each semester. Regardless, for students, report cards offered few surprises. (Parents, on the other hand, may have seen it differently.) Because report cards provided grades in several subjects, students learned their strengths and capabilities, as well as their weaknesses, from the "scorecards."

As leaders, we must recognize that our best team members crave success and need objective validation. Providing timely, actionable, data-based feedback will not only make your best better; it will tell you who won't or can't improve. Winners need to improve. Winners seek promotions, raises, bonuses, and greater opportunities, and they expect leaders to show them how to improve and get things they want. Conversely, losers hate feedback, and they either seek the status quo or operate with a sense of entitlement, expecting to receive promotions, raises, bonuses, and greater opportunities regardless of their performance.

One way to drive away high performers from your team is to provide stale feedback. Just as the purpose of grading assignments in school is providing students timely and actionable feedback, if teachers withheld grades on all tests and projects until after submitting report cards, feedback would not improve learning. The sooner your team receives feedback, the faster they can improve. Serve the feedback hot. Stale and cold feedback, like food, never gets consumed or digested. High performers crave the nourishment of constant, timely feedback.

The only feedback more toxic than stale feedback is factually inaccurate feedback. As a leader I lose credibility when I post incorrect data about team and individual performance. It's the equivalent of sending HQ a "false report." Unfortunately, I have made this mistake from time to time.

Shortly after I launched digital scoreboards across our office that displayed employees' performance metrics, I learned the data did not always accurately transfer from our software programs to the scoreboards. Thus, the scoreboards reflected inaccurate data from time to time. When the inaccurate data appeared on the scoreboards, visibly upset top performers marched into my office and reported my broken program. Sometimes top performers would barge in and tell me that we erroneously published "last week's numbers" again.

The stale and inaccurate data once resulted in a revolt by a leader who removed the power source to the scoreboard, turning the screens off. Ironically, my failure, which bred distrust in the scoreboard, ultimately motivated several leaders to pay attention to their own numbers to ensure accuracy. When the screens turned back on, accountability and attention to metrics soared throughout the organization. The winners held us accountable because they had a primal need to see their names on the leaderboards.

The team members whose names did not appear on the leaderboard said nothing. I'm not sure whether it was because they didn't care about the boards, didn't know their metrics, or felt ashamed of their performance. At first, I didn't know how to address those who did not achieve leaderboard status. I didn't want team members to feel like failures just because they didn't perform well enough to appear on the leaderboard. I addressed it this way: "It's okay with me that you are not on the leaderboard, but the absence of your name from the leaderboard should not be okay with you."

Had we not prioritized fixing the scoreboards, the stale and unreliable data would have killed the credibility of the leaderboards and the leadership team.

WINNERS SEEK FEEDBACK

How do I get better? The best soldiers always wanted to get better, and they never stopped asking how. The soldiers who maxed their PT test wanted to know how high they could score on the "extended scale" and would constantly train to get an even higher score on the next test. The soldiers who shot "expert" at the range wanted to qualify with even more weapons systems or go to sniper school. What impressed me most about these soldiers was not their consistent excellent results, but their shameless drive to become even better and their hunger to be coached.

On the opposite end of the spectrum, the low performers never sought feedback; they fought feedback. They chose to feel offended by feedback rather than inspired. Sometimes written counseling statements opened their eyes, but most of the time they didn't. When I counseled noncommissioned officers and officers who failed to meet the standard, I reminded them of their leadership role and the number of soldiers they led. For the winners, that was enough to change their behavior and raise their standards. For the persistent stragglers, no amount of remedial training, feedback, listening, or wall-to-wall counseling could change their attitude, and thus nothing I could do would change their behavior.

When team members bristle at the feedback you're giving, it's generally because they don't trust your motivation. They assume your purpose is to blame, shame, or belittle, not to motivate, encourage, or develop. Overcoming this misconception takes skill but builds the strongest teams.

DANGEROUS FEEDBACK

While feedback is a gift, it can be a useless gift. Always consider the source and the motives. Great feedback is priceless, but bad feedback is worthless.

Some of the best feedback I received in the military came from commanders who asked questions like: Are you sure you want to do that? Is this the outcome you envisioned? Is that the best you can do? Did you conduct precombat inspections? What does your platoon sergeant think about your plan? Did you get accountability of all your sensitive items? Do you have accountability of all your soldiers? What the f*ck were you thinking?

I have found that the more forceful the feedback, the more likely the person providing it has an ulterior motive. When someone says, "You need to . . . ," beware. When someone says, "Your only option is . . . ," they may not want you to consider other options.

One of my first memories as a new lieutenant was trying to find my assigned company. When I arrived at the company area, the only person present was the CQ. After a phone call and a couple of hours, the first sergeant's driver, a private named Polete, picked me up in a Humvee and drove me from the company area to the firing range. Polete appeared professional, clean cut, and sharp. (In fact, he would later become a highly decorated Special Forces soldier.)

At the range, another junior enlisted soldier awaited my arrival. This soldier held the rank of specialist (paygrade E-4). Although his pay grade and rank were higher than the private who had initially driven me to the range, I could tell his career would look nothing like that of the first sergeant's driver. This was my first encounter with the boss of the E-4 mafia.

For the sake of this story, we can call this soldier "Specialist Stan." Stan had been in the army for nearly a decade. Now, most people who have been enlisted for a decade have reached the rank of, at the very least, sergeant. A person who spends a decade in any career is sure to rise in the ranks at least a little bit. But not this specialist. Apparently, Specialist Stan had made it to the rank of sergeant several times but had his stripes revoked because of violations, insubordination, and general stupidity.

Specialist Stan wasn't a bad guy. In fact, most of the junior enlisted soldiers looked up to him. He maintained proficiency with his weapons systems, he knew all the regulations, he told great stories, and he owned a Harley-Davidson.

However, at least once per month, Stan would do something to ruin any progress he'd made in his career. Stan loved to live in the barracks, even ten years into his military career. He liked the attention that he gained from the new soldiers who looked up to him. On weekends, he often took them around base— and off base—to have fun. Stan also showed soldiers how to get away with shirking their duties, how to bullshit the first sergeant, and how to do the bare minimum to get by. Over the years, Specialist Stan became a cancer to the company. Stan constantly gave feedback in the form of bad advice, whining, and subversive behavior. Stan gave his best advice on how to sham out of a detail.

Unfortunately, many soldiers and leaders fell victim to Stan's eloquent bullshit. Stan's feedback came in the form of a self-serving compliment to his peers, or a veiled attack on the leadership.

We all know people like Stan, and they seldom act alone. In every military unit, a few junior enlisted soldiers who talk about career advancement but never advance gain influence in the organization through their longevity and perceived experience. They use their influence to steer others down the wrong path.

It only takes one Specialist Stan to develop an entire E-4 mafia of bad influences in your unit. The same can be said about your private organization in the civilian world. There are plenty of bad seeds, and it only takes one to begin to spread negativity disguised as feedback throughout an organization.

Sometimes civilian "Karen" would spread gossip in the form of feedback to inoculate herself from her true intention of stirring up drama. In one instance, we rolled out a new expensive employee benefits package. After a year, we requested feedback about the improved benefits from the entire team at a town hall meeting. Karen provided public "feedback" in the form of mischaracterizations about the benefits. At first, we gave her the benefit of the doubt and assumed she misunderstood. After a few questions, it became clear that Karen's negative and inaccurate feedback was baseless. She simply wanted to hijack the venue to stir the pot because she had received a negative performance review the prior week. A leadership team's openness to feedback can be crucial for retention, but a disgruntled employee's weaponized feedback designed to misinform employees about their benefits can be catastrophic if not shut down promptly.

Sometimes the best way to deal with toxic feedback is to address it head-on. Show the team the truth, and then publicly ask for real feedback so the team can see you care about their constructive feedback and will not entertain any attempts to sabotage the feedback loop.

VENDOR FEEDBACK

Initial meetings with vendors usually start off transactional. Their highly trained sales professional listens to your problem and then, magically, their product or service is the only logical solution. Lucky you! The first person you called has the exact solution you need. No need to look any further.

I have found that if you are trying to find the right channels for your marketing campaigns, every vendor has the answer. If you ask a social media company how to grow your company, they will tell you that you need to spend more money on social media. If you ask a search engine optimization company how to get more leads, they will tell you that you need to spend more on SEO. It doesn't matter whether the marketing company or advertising agency sells billboards, TV commercials, radio ads, OTT, PPC, online directories, or yellow page ads, the feedback they give is that your marketing plan needs their services to succeed.

Seeking feedback from vendors almost always results in the vendor telling you that you need their product. The key is not to seek advice from vendors, but a relationship. Once you develop a relationship with your vendors, they often become invested in your success. As they see your company grow, they will want you to be their best testimonial video. They will want to claim a role in your success. Over the years, some of the best feedback and advice I received from vendors was referrals to other companies that provided services I needed that the vendor did not perform. Simply put, the vendor wanted me to succeed.

In some cases, you may develop friendships with vendors. You will know the feedback is genuine the day the vendor tells you your business has outgrown their optimal support level, but they want to continue to support you in your mission even after the transactional relationship ends. I had this relationship with a company called Cathcap, which acted as our fractional CFO as we tripled in size during a period of rapid growth. During a monthly meeting after reviewing all our financial reports, our fractional CFO asked if she could schedule a meeting with Brooke, the CEO of Cathcap. Brooke and I had been friends for years. If I wanted to have an owner-to-owner phone call, I would just call her cell. I found it strange that we would have a formal meeting. Brooke and her team exceeded expectations and played a huge role in our success, so I assumed the purpose of the formal call meant a rate increase.

During the scheduled meeting, Brooke said, "In the beginning of our relationship, I told you we could provide you the most value in the revenue range you specified as your goal. Congratulations, you've achieved that goal faster than you expected and you're ready to bring this capability in-house. Let us know if you need help finding somebody." It felt like the time I turned sixteen and my pediatric dentist fired me because I needed an adult dentist. Brooke and I have remained friends. We collaborate on business ideas, and she provides me great feedback and insights today, free of charge.

AFTER-ACTION REVIEW

Sustain

1. Feedback is a gift, especially when it hurts.

2. The value of the feedback is often directly proportional to the performance level of the person delivering it.

3. Accurate and objective data often provides your most honest feedback.

Improve

1. Always consider the motive of the person/organization/vendor giving feedback. Are they trying to help or trying to sell?

2. Untimely and unreliable data may be worse than inaccurate; it may be misleading.

3. Accurate data and regular feedback don't guarantee you won't make bad leadership decisions from time to time.

16

TASKS, CONDITIONS, AND STANDARDS

The standard you walk past is the standard you accept.

—Attributed to General David Hurley

When it comes to delegation, delegating to a competent, highly trained, and highly motivated team or team member only gets you one step closer. You must ensure that you provide your team with adequate time to execute. You must clearly articulate the task(s), conditions, and standards. Finally, you must have the brains and the guts to hold the team to the standards you set.

Remember the one-third/two-thirds rule mentioned earlier in the book? That's where you allow yourself one-third of the available time to plan, allotting your team the remaining two-thirds of the time to prepare for and complete their plan. If Wednesday morning you receive a mission that must be briefed to the entire organization by close of business on Friday, you must complete your plan and brief key leaders no later than close of business Wednesday so that your team has two days (two-thirds of the time) to complete and brief their plan.

As a civilian I often failed to follow this rule. I spent days succinctly drafting every aspect of the flawless plan. I meticulously briefed every aspect of its execution including contingencies. Then I allowed my teams a few hours to plan and execute. When my teams failed, I blamed the leaders for not preparing. How could they fail to execute this idiot-proof plan? The leaders fired back that they did not have enough time to prepare.

For some reason I could not understand that the one-third/two thirds rule applied to all planning, not just the military. This changed when I started hiring experienced leaders. I soon found that the more senior the leader, the less planning I needed to do. However, I also learned, painfully, that allocating enough time for your team to react and plan doesn't absolve you of your responsibility to set crystal clear expectations.

Your planning must precisely define the tasks, conditions, and standards for your objectives. You as the leader paint the picture for what success looks like. As you articulate your vision of the battle, ensure the entire team can see the operation unfold in their own minds. Don't just tell them your intent; show them.

Descriptively list the specific tasks that you want the team to accomplish. Then state the conditions under which the leader or team will accomplish the mission. Where will the team be working, when, what resources will be available to them, and what constraints should they expect? Finally, succinctly state your standards, and show them what success looks like. Is success 90 percent completion or 100 percent completion? If you can accept losses or delays, your team needs to know. If you *cannot* accept any losses or delays, the team needs to know that as well.

Of course, even if you choose the right leader or team and clearly define the tasks, conditions, and standards, you may still fail. If your well-briefed team lacks adequate training, you, as the leader, may need to remain present to supervise. Furthermore, when you delegate a mission to a team that's experienced, but inexperienced in the task you want accomplished, they won't likely hit the target center-mass the first time. However, the right leader will achieve the standard with minimal corrections. It's like zeroing a weapon at the firing range. The first few rounds won't likely land center-mass on your target, but you will eventually get there after a few small corrections.

Conversely, when you delegate a task or role to a less experienced team, the first attempts may seem more like an artillery exercise. Fire for effect! As you supervise, you will make significant corrections for the team to land a round in the vicinity of the target. Your team will not perform the task as well as or better than you right away, so manage your expectations and theirs. Sometimes close is good enough, especially when you rain steel on a massive target. Sure, you could have done it better yourself. But can you do it better when you're sick? Can you do it better when you're on vacation? Can you do it better when you're not there because you're solving a bigger problem?

Your team improves through experience and repetition. Help

them adjust fire, and they will learn how to hit the targets you set. With your feedback and leadership, inexperienced teams grow into competent teams.

CLARITY: LET YOUR TEAM HELP YOU FIND THE FAULTS IN YOUR PLAN

Did you let your team participate in telling you what could go wrong with your plan? In the military we prepared for every possible scenario during "red hat" planning, where we analyzed the plan from the enemy's point of view. We took the time to assess the enemy's composition, disposition, and strength. The red hat planner played the role of the enemy commander and talked through how they would fight the fight if truly in charge of that unit. As an example, we might assign the red hat planner four IEDs, two RPGs, and twelve enemy combatants, and, through role-play, discover weaknesses and opportunities.

Amazing insights came from these discussions as a fellow officer or NCO talked about where and how they would confront our friendly forces plan. This exercise identified our vulnerabilities throughout the mission. Where are the natural choke points you failed to address during your map reconnaissance? Where could someone most easily ambush you? When we see the battlefield through the eyes of the enemy, we improve our readiness. By the time we completed the red hat exercise, the company commander could prepare for any contingency with clarity.

Remember the back brief? After you walked the team through a five-paragraph operations order, repeated the mission statement twice, showed your team the entire execution on a sand table, and after you asked for questions? "No questions, good, let's start the back brief. Alpha team leader, what are your team's actions on the objective?"

And after the back brief, if you had enough time, you sought even more clarity by conducting rehearsals. You walked through the most important aspects of the operation with the entire team. Everybody talked or walked through their actions at each phase of the operation. The rehearsals helped synchronize actions and raised questions, which refined the plan.

And of course, for the routine enemy encounters, you conducted your battle drills so frequently that the team knew what actions to take if the enemy executed its most dangerous course of action or an unexpected event occurred.

CONDUCT REHEARSALS FOR BOTH FAMILIAR AND UNFAMILIAR

During my deployment to Bosnia, our heavily rehearsed infantry battle drills were replaced with peacekeeping battle drills. Initially our peacekeeping rehearsals seemed insufficient to prepare for civilians on the battlefield (COBs) in heavily populated areas, especially when the COBs intermingled with enemy combatants. We conducted multiple training events in which actors played the role of either civilian or combatant disguised in civilian clothes. As we conducted training patrols, the actors called us names, threw trash at us, grabbed at our weapons, spat at us, and tried to knock us to the ground—all simulating a hostile crowd.

As we went through the scenarios, we saw how an aggressive response would only agitate the crowd. The actors successfully baited many of our soldiers into overreacting and getting into fights with them. Other times, a team of enemy combatants intermingled with the mob of protestors would abduct one of our soldiers. We improved at discerning between a perceived threat and a real threat. Rehearsing different scenarios at full speed with actors who stayed in character ensured that the first time we experienced a hostile crowd we would not be taken by surprise. While we never perfected our responses in training, we improved, and we deployed to Bosnia confident in our abilities.

In the army, we trained more than just about every civilian organization, but we never executed a flawless mission. In the business world, time and resources allocated for training are even more limited. Most businesses spend a majority of their budgeted training time and dollars on their core competencies. Prior to our deployment to Bosnia, our mission was to close with and destroy the enemy. Peacekeeping seemed like a mission for a civil affairs unit, not an infantry platoon. However, several years later, in Iraq, every deploying unit rehearsed similar techniques to handle an intermixed population of civilians and combatants.

In business, it seems strange that we would ever need training outside our core mission. For example, if you run a logistics company, you're likely more worried about the efficiency of your transportation, quality of your drivers, supply discipline, and customer service than you are about HR protocol. Sure, you'll invest in training your people to use their equipment, but you're never going to waste time walking through your HR procedures, right?

If you deployed, you probably remember the tactical standard operating procedures (TACSOP). The TACSOP booklet contained all your battle drills and just about any action you needed to take. I don't recall ever reading the S-1 (military version of human resources) section of the TACSOP. I'm not saying it didn't exist, but I never read it.

The problem with documented administrative policies and procedures in civilian organizations is that nobody reads them until they need to take action, and when they do, they seldom rehearse the steps before live fire. To be fair, most of these documented policies and procedures rarely get used, so spending valuable training time on them makes little sense to the efficient leader. Sure, some organizations may flirt with reality-based leadership training, but not for every functional area of the business.

If you have an administrative procedure that you haven't used in a while, conduct a walk-through rehearsal first before you try to execute. If you have time, assign actors to role-play the affected individuals as you walk through the steps. You may learn that your written procedures are neither as tight nor as clear as you think.

For example, terminating a team member rarely goes smoothly when it's a secondary duty for one of your leaders. Hence, time permitting, rehearsing the termination procedures before you fire someone is generally a good idea. We don't terminate people often, but when we do, we want team members to leave with dignity, maintaining a friendly social relationship and ideally even business referral relationships. When it comes to terminating a team member, it's not about you—you've already made the heart-wrenching decision—it's about the person leaving who is going to feel the impact of your decision, and you don't want to screw it up for them. How we offboard a team member says as much about the strength of our culture as how we onboard them.

Imagine the following scenario during one of your terminations that you failed to rehearse: The employee that you plan to terminate, "Amy," arrives late to the termination meeting, claiming not to know about the meeting. She looks upset and feels ambushed.

As the termination meeting begins, the IT team simultaneously removes Amy's network access but fails to remove her local access. At the conclusion of the termination, leaders on the termination team fail to escort Amy out of the building. Instead, Amy, visibly upset, storms through the hallway, returns to her office, and slams the door. Confused employees receive an email from HR that Amy, who just walked back into her office, has been terminated. The termination team, believing they completed their mission, go home for the day, leaving Amy in her former office with access to all company devices including laptop, issued cell phone, and client lists.

Amy, now a disgruntled former employee, has ample opportunity to commit the following acts of sabotage:

1. Take all her company-issued IT devices with her on her way out the door

2. Wait until everyone leaves for the day and do as she pleases with the building

3. Download local files from her office desktop

4. Contact other departments unaware of the termination to regain access to the network, sensitive information, and trade secrets

5. Intentionally compromise personal information of team members

While the leaders on your termination team may have participated in multiple terminations in other organizations, have they ever worked together on your team? You may absolutely fail in the execution of a termination because you didn't take the time to walk through everyone's role. Sure, you documented every step, but without a walk-through, the coordination and communication pieces get fuzzy. Now imagine if you made the termination team walk through each step, conducting a rehearsal with key team members, maintaining alignment and synchronization throughout the process.

Terminations are one of several operations that you hope to conduct rarely. However, all operations, even the uncomfortable ones, go a lot smoother when you document the process and rehearse the procedure prior to execution. Without rehearsals we have fumbled through unsynchronized employee onboarding, operating systems updates, and even billing processes. Delivering your team a plan with tasks, conditions, and standards is not enough. You must also rehearse the actions as a team. A quick walk-through will get everyone on the same page and synchronize your efforts. This is the value of military tabletop exercises for walking through how you will resolve problems before they occur, such as IT disasters (power outages or internet security breaches) and serious HR issues. Engaging in war gaming with your staff will not only prepare you to respond to the next crisis but also provide a common understanding among your team and align their efforts.

NEGLIGENT DISCHARGE: ACCOUNTABILITY IN THE ORGANIZATION

Discharging employees is never easy, but you will never have accountability if you permit substandard performance. We must be brutally honest when a team member falls below a standard. Sometimes this can be fixed with retraining, but other more serious conduct requires immediate termination, such as discrimination, sexual harassment, criminal behavior, and unethical conduct. The standard of what requires termination versus corrective action can evolve in an organization.

In 1999, when I deployed to Bosnia, we cleared weapons in a clearing barrel every time we entered Camp Demi, our forward operating base (FOB). To properly clear a weapon utilizing a clearing barrel, you had to eject the magazine, charge the bolt to the rear, inspect the chamber to ensure no rounds remained in the weapon, and dry fire the weapon into the clearing barrel.

Every thirty days or so, a soldier failed to follow procedure and fired a live round into the clearing barrel. At the time, this offense was known as an "accidental discharge." While accidental discharges *could* be punished with an article 15 for the negligent act, the nomenclature for these types of incidents was problematic. Calling an unintended discharge of weapon an "accident" is tantamount to calling a motor vehicle homicide a "mistake."

By the time I deployed to Iraq in 2005, the Department of Defense adjusted the naming convention to more accurately align with its values. The "accidental discharge" received a new, values-driven moniker to reflect the serious nature of the professional warrior. The rebranded "negligent discharge" spoke to accountability and carried a mandatory punishment. Unfortunately, I'm unaware as to whether renaming the offense, and adding teeth to the consequences, resulted in fewer negligent discharges, but it was a step in the right direction.

Yes, accidents happen in every organization. However, one of the best ways to mitigate the risk of accidents is to demonstrate intolerance for the acts likely to cause the "accident." One of the scariest things in the practice of law is a missed deadline. A missed deadline can permanently harm a client's case, resulting in legal malpractice. Sure, you can call a missed deadline an accident, but a missed deadline is also clear negligence. While a missed deadline may originate from a calendaring mistake, a poorly designed docketing system, or an untrained assistant, treating it as an accident fails to convey the serious nature of the offense.

Great organizations learn from mistakes, but they do not tolerate negligence. While you don't have to fire someone every time your organization misses a deadline, you can document it with a formal counseling statement so that the responsible team member understands the potential severity of the problem. Furthermore, even though you may choose to conduct the reprimand in private, your team should be aware that it happened; whether you publicly dime out the employee is your decision. And of course, if your team finds the organization missed a deadline and the leadership did nothing, your team will learn about it, and missed deadlines will become an accepted part of your team culture.

One of the challenges of leading an organization with several teams comes from a misunderstanding of team accountability. From a leadership perspective, you hold the team leaders accountable, and the team leaders hold the individuals in their assigned teams accountable. Sometimes a newly minted senior leader who rose through the ranks instinctively wants to get back in the trenches and fix the problem himself to prevent the team from suffering more failures. Doing this deprives the junior leaders of the opportunity to solve the problem, which ultimately stunts their growth.

When I run into issues like the missed deadline problem, I speak directly with the team lead and ask who was responsible for the deadline. Often the team leader will say, "Me, sir!" But that could be the wrong answer. While the team lead ultimately bears responsibility for the missed deadline, the real question is whether the team lead can identify who, on her team, she charged with the responsibility of meeting the deadline. If the missed deadline arose from a work completion issue, does the leader know why the team member failed to complete the task on time?

If it was a work submission issue, did the person charged with submitting the work receive notice of the deadline? If it was a calendaring issue, who on her team owns the calendar? If it was a training issue, how did we assign a deadline to an untrained team member?

Yes, the missed deadline can be characterized as nothing less than a failure of the team leader. However, at the organizational level, you are solving a problem larger than a missed deadline. You need to ensure missed deadlines are not systematic. In other words, firing the offender won't solve an unidentified systems problem or a leader problem. You don't have the luxury of waiting for another missed deadline to cross your desk to figure out the root problem. Does your subordinate leader tolerate negligence, or does the leader need retraining on delegation?

While unforeseen accidents happen in business, most business "accidents" are foreseeable. You as the leader must vigilantly develop a culture of accountability where leaders take ownership of negligent discharges and don't treat them or label them as "accidents." Your company may be one negligent act away from a lawsuit that drives you into bankruptcy and destroys your company.

AFTER-ACTION REVIEW

Sustain

1. Everyone on the team needs to know your standards. Set crystal clear expectations.

2. Give your leaders enough time to plan.

3. Senior leaders need less guidance from you and more time to plan.

Improve

1. If your team doesn't understand your standards, it's your fault.

2. Leaders must choose standards. More importantly, leaders must enforce those standards.

3. Words matter. You may not be able to prevent "accidents" in your organization, but you can take action to reduce "negligence."

17

KNOWLEDGE DEVELOPMENT

Leadership and learning are indispensable to each other.

—John F. Kennedy, remarks prepared for
Dallas Citizens Council, 1963

The organizational power of the military lies in its commitment to developing its leaders. No military leader spends an entire career doing the same thing. The military develops well-rounded leaders by broadening their experiences throughout their careers. Every officer and noncommissioned officer receives training and new perspectives as students, instructors, or staff members between primary leadership positions.

The civilian sector is no stranger to this concept. Allstate offers several developmental programs, including their Technology Development Leadership Program, which has a three-subject cycle for training workers on technology operations, while also exposing them to business and leadership skills. AmeriCorp follows an 80/20 rule, where 20 percent of their employees'

John swearing in his brother, Rory T. Berry,
upon his commissioning as a navy officer

time is spent on training and self-improvement. Their VISTA program focuses on teaching volunteers project management, collaboration, and leadership skills. Deloitte built Deloitte University, a $300 million learning center dedicated to improving the training, tools, and opportunities of their employees.

In growing our organization, we knew that as a small company we could not develop every team member's technical skills internally. Further, while we felt confident in our ability to develop leaders, we knew we lacked the experience to develop the senior leaders we needed to scale. Finally, as we recruited highly talented lawyers, we learned most wanted to maximize their valuable time practicing law rather than "squandering it" participating in leadership development programs.

While we struggled to find solutions to these problems in the short term, we knew that we could make progress. We faced our constraints and temporarily accepted them as facts. We focused on building a leader development plan with the resources and team we had, rather than wishing for the one we wanted in the future.

First, we created a leadership structure separate from our pay structure. We knew that not all team members wanted to advance to leadership positions. Several technicians joined our company because they saw our leadership model as a resource that could provide them the support necessary to focus on their primary objective, which was to excel in their field and win for their clients. They needed a way to earn more money and gain seniority in the organization without the burden of leadership. On the other hand, we had to fairly compensate leaders who dedicated time to developing their teams at the cost of their individual results. Separating leadership compensation from production compensation made this possible.

Additionally, our compensation structure also allowed team members to participate in leadership roles without risking their careers if they failed. Many people love the *idea* of leading a team, but once they fully experience the burden of leadership, they realize they were much happier and more profitable as a technician. This happens because most highly skilled senior professionals who feel a duty (or entitlement) to lead, don't like to shift focus between leading a team and honing their craft.

Separating pay and seniority from our leadership track seemed to strike the correct balance. It allowed team members to pursue leadership opportunities but opt out after a year if they decided they preferred the role of skilled technician over the role of multifaceted leader.

Like most small businesses, we currently lack the expertise and resources to adequately internally train our team members for some of our growing business functions such as finance, marketing, and technology. We simply lack the size and revenue to build a career path for every team member. Instead, for areas that require specialized knowledge outside of our core competencies, we hire team members willing to forge their own paths and tell us what education and training they need to reach the career progression they desire. We invest in developing these leaders by sending them to certification courses, paying for them to join professional organizations, and in some cases hiring the trainers to come to our office and train them.

For example, our HR director, Reta, started as a paralegal. Her superior management skills earned her an internal promotion to office manager after a few years. As our team grew, she took the initiative to earn her certification as a law firm administrator by an external organization. Two years later, we began to build out the C-suite, which would make her position obsolete when we hired our COO. Reta did not panic about her future but instead decided she would become a member of the C-suite.

She earned her PhD, and we promoted her to director of HR, where she has thrived. Reta pursues professional development throughout the year by participating in national organizations and certification programs that provide continuing education in her functional area of HR. While pathfinders like Reta are rare in the civilian world, they are invaluable to the organization. Reta possesses over a decade of institutional knowledge, and her career proves that opportunity for growth and promotion exists for everyone within our organization.

The more difficult reality to stomach is that when you hire senior leaders into your organization, you can only provide them a growing future if you grow your organization fast enough. It took me almost six months to recruit and hire our COO, Chad. Chad, a former cavalry officer, led a platoon in Iraq and commanded a company in Afghanistan. His degrees included both a JD and an MBA. He had worked for one of the largest financial institutions in the world and one of the fifty largest law firms. I signed him to a three-year term. During the first two years, he built the systems and processes I outlined in our initial counseling faster than expected. While Chad didn't enjoy living in Nebraska, he played all-in every day and fit right into the team culture of excellence and rapid growth.

Just as I was preparing to schedule Chad's second annual review, he walked into my office and told me that he had received an offer to become CEO of a company three times the size of ours in the state where he wanted to live. Surprisingly, I felt proud rather than upset. I had paid a fortune in headhunting fees to secure Chad, and he still had a year left on his contract with our team. However, this meant nothing compared to the joy I felt that one of our own was leaving to command a company three times our size.

In military terms, Chad's role as COO was the equivalent to that of an operations officer (S3). He was the second in command. His next promotion opportunity was either when I stepped down or resigned or when he took command of another company.

In military officership, the common leadership path is staff time, command time, staff time, command time, with the understanding that staff time prepares you for your next command. Chad had succeeded as a staff officer, and it was time for him to take command. I released him from his final year obligation, and we celebrated his upcoming command opportunity. Yes, replacing a second in command would be time consuming, expensive, and challenging. But ultimately this is why we chose to become leaders. We develop others into someone better than the person we met. We develop them into someone better than the person we are, and in doing so, we become better.

YOUR ULTIMATE KNOWLEDGE DEVELOPMENT

Your ultimate knowledge development will not come from a school, leadership position, or a mentor. As the leader of your organization, your ultimate knowledge development is self-knowledge, which you gain only by leading others. Know who you are, and lead from there.

During the three weeks I spent at Gerry Spence's Trial Lawyers College, I learned that the most vulnerable person in the courtroom is the most powerful person there. Similarly, the most vulnerable leader is the most authentic leader. As a veteran, you can smell deception a mile away, and you respect the leaders who have the courage to be authentic.

Often military rigidity seems in conflict with the authentic leader. Shortly before my military retirement, an officer candidate asked me, "How can you adhere to rigid standards and maintain authenticity?" My answer, "When you genuinely care about your team and your mission, you cannot be authentic without enforcing rigid standards."

While we as leaders incessantly think of ways to develop our teams, we must also consider our own development and plot the course to grow as leaders.

AFTER-ACTION REVIEW

Sustain

1. Every leader seeks opportunities for development and advancement.

2. Leader development opportunities exist outside your organization and outside of your industry.

3. Leaders need both breadth and depth of experience to become agile, well-rounded, and wise.

Improve

1. Smaller organizations often lack the expertise and resources to adequately develop team members throughout their entire careers.

2. Your technicians who seek to become world class in their craft often desire advancement opportunities separate from leadership roles.

3. When leaders feel they can no longer grow in your organization, they often leave.

18

RESILIENCE AND COURAGE

Success is how high you bounce when you hit bottom.

—Attributed to George S. Patton

THIS IS THE WETTEST YOU WILL EVER BE

My father tells stories about transporting from fire base to fire base in Vietnam by jeep on permissive travel orders. He had no convoy, no up-armored vehicle, no vehicle roof, not even an assigned gunner—just a driver who carried a grenade launcher and a tiger scout interpreter who carried an M16 rifle. On one occasion, rain poured down into the jeep as the sergeant driver began to lose traction on a primitive jungle road. As the monsoon intensified, the road washed out, and the jeep's wheels got stuck in the mud of what was increasingly looking more like a river than a road. My father, the tiger scout, and the sergeant began walking toward division headquarters in the downpour.

The heavier the rain fell, the more my father complained about getting wet. His complaining grew to encompass the density of the jungle, the distance they had yet to walk, and the lack of a poncho and then went back to the rain. Finally, the sergeant sneered, "Sir, quit your bitching. You're the wettest you'll ever be."

The sergeant's words made my father smile. He couldn't stop the downpour, but he could maintain absolute control over his attitude. The three humped a click before they got out of the rain and even laughed once or twice before arriving at HQ.

When my father volunteered to serve as a JAG officer in Vietnam, he did not expect to walk through the jungle in the rain like an infantry soldier; nor had he prepared to do so. Yet there he was, no poncho, no wet weather gear, breaking the bush of the jungle with feet and hands.

In the military, and in business, the sky opens up and pours on us whether we expect it or not. We initially perceive our plans melting as though we have hit an all-time low, until we realize it's not that bad. Our attitudes as leaders shape how our teams react. Once you get wet, you might as well laugh about it because you can do little else. Most obstacles eventually become opportunities, as long as we treat them as such.

I'm grateful for all the expected and unexpected inclement weather I experienced in the military. Storms may slow our progress, but they don't change the mission or give us permission to lower the standard or change direction. We continue to march toward our objective, rain or shine. The wind that blows in our faces today will be silent tomorrow and at our backs the next.

And let's face it: if you are setting up a patrol base and digging in with your entrenching tool, it's a lot easier to dig dirt when it's wet. Sometimes the storm is a blessing.

I've had days as a leader when I made so many poor decisions and mistakes that the organization would have been better off if I had stayed home. I've also had days when, despite my performance, fate dealt the team a major blow that we did not foresee. In business, like life, we head into the storm face-first like the buffalo on the prairie.

As leaders, we must decisively react to the storms, because tiny heart syndrome—an outward manifestation of whining, weakness, and lack of accountability—becomes contagious. If the leader loses confidence and picks out the negative in everything, others will follow suit. Soon either the team loses confidence in the leader or, worse, the team embodies the leader's negative attitude.

There will always be points in life when you are the wettest you will ever be. At some point, bad press can't get any worse, key clients fire you, best team members quit, bet-the-company strategies fail. When we find ourselves in the rain, without shelter, sometimes we just have to endure being wet until the sun comes out and dries us off.

The key is knowing the difference in when to suck it up and drive on and when to use the liquid sunshine to your advantage. In the words of Roger Miller, "Some people feel the rain; others just get wet."[1] Leaders who can feel out the root problem start looking for solutions. Leaders who focus on getting wet, beaten, or bloodied panic and demoralize their teams in the process.

In business, you may find yourself in the middle of a pandemic, a recession, a data breach, a lawsuit, and a power outage all at once. How will your team respond? How will you respond? Most importantly, how will your competitors respond? If your entire industry suffers a catastrophic event, most everyone faces the same disadvantages. Leaders see opportunity. If current events have weakened my position, so too have my competitors been weakened. Strike now!

LTC John S. Berry looking forward to a bigger future after completing twenty years of combined active and reserve duty

IF YOU ARE ALREADY A LEADER, IT'S TOO LATE TO QUIT

Everyone who joined the military remembers that moment when it was too late to quit. For some, it was the first day at boot camp. Once you got off the bus and the drill sergeant started yelling, you couldn't just say, "Enough! I quit." If you did that, you would only draw more fire to yourself and those around you, and the drill sergeants would have delighted in inflicting pain on your team members while you contemplated your words.

"Oh, you want to quit? Great, let me get you some milk and cookies while we arrange for your limousine. In the meantime, PVT Snuffy will hold your duffel bag over his head until the limo gets here to ensure it stays dry and clean. PVT Jones"— who is already in the push-up position—"will provide your seat so you can wait comfortably. Go ahead and sit on his back while you wait."

I know some civilians reading this book right now are thinking, "If the drill sergeant did that, I would tell him to stop immediately, report the drill sergeant's conduct to his commanding officer, and demand a congressional inquiry into the hazing." Sure you would.

And another civilian is thinking, "This doesn't sound like leadership to me; this is cruel and uncalled for. This is the antithesis of leadership." Well, you're right, the shakedown at boot camp or basic training does not teach you how to lead. It teaches you how to survive. If you cannot survive, you cannot lead. No person leads from the grave.

People don't just quit during bad times; they also quit during successful times. The year we crossed the threshold into eight figures, we had not only doubled our revenue from two years prior but also doubled in size, with plans to grow even larger and much faster. Amid the excitement and chaos of rapid growth, one of our senior team members asked to meet with me outside of the office. "John, I need to talk to you about something." I expected this was about our new office location, a recent hire, or a request for a raise.

"Chuck" showed up at my house at 9:00 a.m. on a Saturday. As soon as he walked in the front door, he blurted out, "I'll get to the point. I'm proud of where the organization is going; I just don't want to be part of it."

I didn't know how to respond. How could Chuck not want to be on the team anymore? Chuck explained that he enjoyed the team and his role most when we had ten employees. Not only did rapid growth exhaust him, but the team, mission, and culture had all changed. He wanted to be a part of a smaller team again. I missed those days too, but it was too late to quit. I couldn't go back.

Once you commit to growing an organization, it's too late to quit and reverse course. If you don't embrace the growth you initiated, you fail all those team members and their families who count on you for more pay, more opportunities, and a better future. You promised a stable future through organizational growth, and a change of course would send panic through the organization.

As a soldier, getting comfortable being uncomfortable becomes a way of life. Horrible heat rash, blisters on your feet, lesions on your back from your rucksack, and losing feeling in your extremities while you shiver never morph into excuses for failing a mission. We brag about adversity and discomfort after we complete the mission.

Leaders tend to show their colors when facing discomfort. They step into the spotlight and offer everybody hope. They don't let the team quit. This is where the military veteran shines.

We know what it's like to be tired, hungry, exhausted, disappointed, and sad, all while being away from our families. We know what it's like to endure physical pain. We know what it's like not to have the assets we need to accomplish the mission at hand. We know what it's like to be assigned an unsavory mission. Most of all, we know to move forward, regardless of the circumstances. We know how to see the upside of things, regardless of how dark the immediate future may seem.

When you grow in your civilian role and achieve an even bigger future than you ever thought possible, remember this: there will be times when you would give anything to trade in your top-floor corner office to get back down in the dirt with the maniacal bunch who taught you how to lead.

When I was ten years old, I became a paper boy. Getting up early in the morning and delivering papers in the rain or snow never bothered me. Alone, I focused on my work. I didn't complain about the weather because I had no one to complain to. The sleeping world didn't care. At thirteen years old, I started a second job detasseling corn. I worked alongside people who rode the bus to the farm, hated their jobs, and spoke of nothing but getting back on the bus at the end of the day and going home. Their negativity became infectious. The complaining started as we waited for the bus to arrive, continued on the bus, and could be heard through the rows of corn as we worked.

One day, when it was so hot and dry that the corn stock cut us even though we were wearing long sleeves, I watched my smiling supervisor walk up and down the rows. During a break I asked, "Why are you so happy? Everybody else is miserable. They just want to get back on the bus and go home."

The supervisor's smile grew just a bit wider, and he said, "Someday, when you grow up, you'll know this, but there are plenty of days when I wish I was back in these fields. I did this job when I was your age and I dreaded it." He went on to tell me that he had made plenty of money at this point in his life and no longer needed this type of work, but he did it every summer to reset his perspective on life. "I'm doing this job because it's better than some of the days I have in my air-conditioned office," he said.

Tough times never end and, as leaders, we seek them out. Once we stop looking to solve bigger problems, we stop leading, and the team abandons us to find a real leader. The leadership journey brings us to several low points. When you're the wettest you will ever be, you can stay stuck in the mud or you can move toward your goals. It's your choice.

AFTER-ACTION REVIEW

Sustain

1. You've handled adversity in the military; you already know how to move forward.

2. You've succeeded under less favorable conditions in the past.

3. Enjoy the discomfort; it's part of the journey.

Improve

1. Once you commit, it's too late to quit.

2. Your attitude sets the tone for your organization.

3. Complaining to your team won't make anything better.

CONCLUSION

*What has been will be again, what has been done will be
done again; there is nothing new under the sun.*

—Ecclesiastes 1:9 (NIV)

Your military leadership knowledge and experience are the
result of thousands of years of planning, iterating, and adapting by those who served before you. The universal nature of
leadership makes your military experience invaluable. Leadership
is a transferable skill, and those who served know it best.

The more I study, read, and learn, the more I am convinced
that there is nothing new under the sun. You already know what
you need to know. You learned it all in the military. You didn't
need to read this book, or any book, to know what you learned
through your military experience. You don't need anyone to tell
you. You already know the one thing that must be experienced
to be understood; you know real leadership.

I didn't write this book to tell you what I know, I wrote it to
remind you of what you already know and encourage you to use
that knowledge and experience.

Your military experience is the key that unlocks your bigger future. While all businesses are basically the same, they are also vastly different, even within the same niche industry. There is no "right way" to run your organization, just as there is no "right way" to lead. You choose both your destination and your path. Perhaps you may experience even more success if you do the opposite of everything I suggest in this book. I only know what worked for me and what didn't.

I hope that these recollections of my experiences reminded you of your own, or, at the very least, that you learned some cheap lessons from my failures. I have accomplished nothing extraordinary, nothing that other veteran business owners have not already done. I served. I learned from my military service. I applied those lessons with the help of many other leaders. I am proud of my team.

On my journey I learned that every theory or lesson comes in several flavors and occurs repeatedly. An author adds a new slant and repackages the same basic tenets with a flashy title, disguising unoriginal thoughts and lessons with unnecessary drivel. Perhaps I have done the same. What worked for me may not work for you. I also make room for the possibility that I may be completely wrong as to why I succeeded at times and why I failed. When we pursue a specific result, we learn what works and what does not work, but the "why" can be illusive.

To lead means to care. Many of us were told that to be a successful military leader, you need to know your soldiers and always place their needs above your own, as our NCOs do. This is equally true in the civilian sector. Know your team members. Be engaged in their lives. Support and promote their success, and your organization will experience success.

I hear business coaches and gurus talk about the importance of not becoming emotionally invested in your business. They preach that you should not seek personal fulfillment from your organization but focus on financial profit. These "coaches" never served in the military and have never shouldered the burden of protecting the futures of America's sons and daughters.

If you served, you've developed the skills to succeed in your post-military leadership objectives, whatever they may be. More importantly, you've proven you care enough to make a difference in the lives of others. In this book, we discuss some of those skills that may help. More important than any of the skills in this book, however, are the courage and relentless resilience you learned in the military. Joining the military takes courage; leading in the military takes even more courage. As a civilian leader, you will draw on that courage through your many failures and challenges. What is most important is that you know from your military service that you have what it takes to overcome those obstacles.

Leadership matters most when the obvious response is to quit. John C. Maxwell said, "You can easily determine the caliber of a person by the amount of opposition it takes to discourage him or her."[1] I always liked that. Embrace the suck, never surrender, never admit defeat. Fight on to achieve the objective no matter what.

Military leaders know what they must do to win, and they develop their training plans accordingly. In any fight, the enemy has a vote, and therefore plans must be adaptable to change. Your sergeants prepared you in ways a civilian could never fathom. The training you received in the military allowed you to serve your country to your greatest ability, and now it allows you to turn around and serve your community and its people.

The moment you receive your DD-214, a new world of opportunity opens up to you. The potential for affecting the lives of others changes when you no longer surround yourself with comrades who have similar, or superior, training. Ironically, when your military service ends, your community needs you more than ever. Regardless of your branch or rank, or whether you served in peace time or in combat, people look up to you.

Employ the principles that were embedded in you as a member of the armed forces and teach them to others. Demonstrate your leadership abilities to others who might not have them, and teach them how to be leaders themselves. You already know how.

As you navigate life, holding these military values with you, remember that while you don't consider yourself a hero, those around you do. Your family, friends, colleagues, and anyone else who enters your life can become better people from your example of service.

Go out and be the hero to those you want to serve.

To listen to the *Veteran Led* podcast, scan the following QR code or search "Veteran Led" on your favorite listening platform.

To learn more about how Berry Law helps veterans, scan the following QR code.

ACKNOWLEDGMENTS

Special thanks go to the Grim Reapers of A Co. 1-5 CAV, who taught me many of the leadership lessons in this book. I owe content credit and leadership development lessons to Chad Collins, who not only helped with parts of the book but also made the Berry Law vision come true. My executive assistant, Betsy Armatys, was the driving force behind not only the completion of this book but the entire Veteran Led movement. Most importantly, this book would not exist without the bravery and dedication to justice of my father, founder of Berry Law John Stevens Berry Sr. Finally, I could not have written this book without the support of the Berry Law team, who defend the United States Constitution every day, one client at a time.

NOTES

CHAPTER 2

1. BambooHR, "First Impressions Are Everything: 44 Days to Make or Break a New Hire," accessed May 2024, https://www.bamboohr.com/resources/guides/onboarding-statistics-2023.

2. Dawn Klinghoffer, Candice Young, and Dave Haspas, "Every New Employee Needs an Onboarding 'Buddy,'" *Harvard Business Review*, June 6, 2019, https://hbr.org/2019/06/every-new-employee-needs-an-onboarding-buddy?registration=success.

3. Irina Ivanova, "Former Equifax CEO Testifies before House Energy Committee—as It Happened," *CBS News*, October 3, 2017, https://www.cbsnews.com/live-news/former-equifax-ceo-testifies-congress-richard-smith/.

4. Mandy Stephenson, "Here's Why If You Never Fail, You're Doing It Wrong," Combat Flip Flops, July 11, 2016, https://www.combatflipflops.com/blogs/combat-flip-flops/here-s-why-if-you-never-fail-you-re-doing-it-wrong.

5. Confucius, "The Analects," *Internet Classics Archive*, accessed May 29, 2024, https://classics.mit.edu/Confucius/analects.1.1.html.

6. Robert Solano, phone interview by the author, May 21, 2023. All quotations attributed to Solano in this section are from this interview.

7. G. K. Chesterton, "Christmas and Disarmament," in *The Collected Works of G. K. Chesterton*, vol. 29, *The Illustrated London News, 1911–1913*, ed. Lawrence J. Clipper (San Francisco: Ignatius Press, 1988), 22.

CHAPTER 3

1. Jon Dick, "Live Chat Exposes a Fatal Flaw in Your Go-to-Market," *HubSpot* (blog), January 19, 2021, https://blog .hubspot.com/sales/live-chat-go-to-market-flaw.

2. Ryan Baum, "22 Live Chat Statistics You Need to Know in 2023," *Gorgias*, October 4, 2023, https://www.gorgias .com/blog/live-chat-statistics#toc-1-86-of-live-chat-tickets -end-with-a-satisfied-customer.

3. Katherine Haan, "Top Website Statistics for 2024," *Forbes Advisor*, April 2, 2024, https://www.forbes.com/advisor/ business/software/website-statistics/.

4. Aaron De Smet, Marino Mugayar-Baldocchi, Angelika Reich, and Bill Schaninger, "Some Employees Are Destroying Value. Others Are Building It. Do You Know the Difference?" *McKinsey Quarterly*, September 11, 2023, https://www.mckinsey.com/capabilities/people -and-organizational-performance/our-insights/some -employees-are-destroying-value-others-are-building -it-do-you-know-the-difference.

5. Rinku Thakkar, "Top 100 Hiring Statistics for 2022," LinkedIn, July 16, 2022, https://www.linkedin.com/pulse/ top-100-hiring-statistics-2022-rinku-thakkar/.

6. Courtney Kube and Molly Boigon, "Every Branch of the Military Is Struggling to Make Its 2022 Recruiting Goals, Officials Say," *NBC News*, June 27, 2022, https://www .nbcnews.com/news/military/every-branch-us-military -struggling-meet-2022-recruiting-goals-officia-rcna35078.

7. George S. Patton Jr., *War as I Knew It* (Boston: Houghton Mifflin, 1995), 354.

CHAPTER 4

1. Cameron Herold, phone interview/coaching call with the author, February 2021.

CHAPTER 5

1. Brendan Ballou, *Plunder: Private Equity's Plan to Pillage America* (New York: Hatchette Book Group, 2023), 66.

2. Ballou, *Plunder*, 34.

3. Brendan Ballou, "When Private-Equity Firms Bankrupt Their Own Companies," *The Atlantic*, May 1, 2023, https://www.theatlantic.com/ideas/archive/2023/05/ private-equity-firms-bankruptcies-plunder-book/673896/.

4. Americans for Financial Reform, "Fact Sheet: Stop Private Equity from Driving Retailers into Bankruptcy, Destroying Jobs and Livelihoods," October 19, 2021, https:// ourfinancialsecurity.org/2021/10/fact-sheet-stop -private-equity-from-driving-retailers-into-bankruptcy -destroying-jobs-and-livelihoods/.

5. Patrick M. Malone, *The Skulking Way of War: Technology and Tactics among the New England Indians* (Lanham, MD: Madison Books, 2000).

CHAPTER 6

1. James Clear, "The Ivy Lee Method: The Daily Routine Experts Recommend for Peak Productivity," *James Clear*, accessed May 29, 2024, https://jamesclear.com/ivy-lee.
2. Claire Sibonney, "Arianna Huffington on the Third Metric: You Can Complete a Project by Dropping It," *HuffPost*, September 11, 2013, https://www.huffpost.com/archive/ca/entry/arianna-huffington-on-the-third-metric-you-can-complete-a-proje_n_3901302.
3. Jeff Southerland, *Scrum: The Art of Doing Twice the Work in Half the Time* (New York: Crown, 2014).

CHAPTER 7

1. Keith J. Cunningham, *The Road Less Stupid: Advice from the Chairman of the Board* (Austin, TX: Keys to the Vault, 2017), 25–26.
2. Carley Knobloch, "Why the Keurig KOLD Failed," *Carley K.*, June 22, 2016, https://carleyk.com/uncategorized/keurig-kold-failed; Mary Ellen Shoup, "Price, Size, and Consumer Audience Led to Failure of Keurig Kold, Euromonitor Analyst Says," *Beverage Daily*, June 9, 2016, https://www.beveragedaily.com/Article/2016/06/10/Price-size-and-consumer-audience-led-to-failure-of-Keurig-Kold; Christopher Doering, "Inside Keurig's Evolution from Single-Serve Novelty to Coffee Powerhouse," *Food Dive*, February 12, 2024, https://www.fooddive.com/news/keurig-coffee-evolution-from-single-serve-novelty-to-brewer-of-coffeehouse/701854.

CHAPTER 8

1. Jeffrey K. Liker, *The Toyota Way: 14 Management Principles from the World's Greatest Manufacturer* (New York: McGraw Hill, 2004).

CHAPTER 9

1. Atul Gawande, *The Checklist Manifesto: How to Get Things Right* (New York: Metropolitan Books, 2009).

CHAPTER 10

1. George S. Patton Jr., *War as I Knew It* (Boston: Houghton Mifflin, 1995), 354.

CHAPTER 11

1. Carl von Clausewitz, "Friction in War," in *On War*, vol. 1, trans. J. J. Graham (London: N. Trübner, 1873), clausewitzstudies.org, accessed May 26, 2024, https://www.clausewitzstudies.org/readings/OnWar1873/BK1ch07.html.

CHAPTER 12

1. Jim Collins, *Good to Great: Why Some Companies Make the Leap . . . and Others Don't* (New York: Harper Business, 2001).

2. Simon Sinek, *Leaders Eat Last: Why Some Teams Pull Together and Others Don't* (New York: Portfolio, 2014), 24.

3. Jason Fitzgerald, "Roster Turnover in the NFL," *Over the Cap*, April 19, 2022, https://overthecap.com/roster-turnover-in-the-nfl.

4. John Schuhmann, "Continuity Rankings: Breaking Down Each Team's Roster Turnover," NBA, December 3, 2020, https://www.nba.com/news/continuity-rankings-2020-21-season.

5. Rob Mains, "Flu-Like Symptoms: Change Agents—Why Roster Turnover Has Skyrocketed," *Baseball Prospectus*, March 4, 2019, https://www.baseballprospectus.com/news/article/47548/flu-like-symptoms-change-agents-why-roster-turnover-has-skyrocketed/.

CHAPTER 18

1. "'King of the Road' Roger Miller Wears No Special Labels except He's Talented," *Lubbock Avalanche-Journal*, December 31, 1972, p. 5.

CONCLUSION

1. John C. Maxwell, *Running with the Giants: What the Old Testament Heroes Want You to Know about Life and Leadership* (Nashville, TN: FaithWorks, 2002), 115.

ABOUT THE AUTHOR

 **JOHN S. BERRY** is a highly accomplished attorney, an army veteran, and a passionate advocate for empowering his fellow veterans. His multifaceted career has been defined by exceptional leadership, service, and an unwavering commitment to fighting for those who have served their country.

Berry's military journey began when he received his commission as an infantry officer in the U.S. Army after graduating from the College of William and Mary. He completed Airborne School and Ranger School and deployed to Bosnia in 1999 for Operation Joint Forge as a platoon leader. Berry also served as a company commander during Operation Iraqi Freedom in Iraq. He finished his military career as a battalion commander in the Nebraska Army National Guard, retiring as a lieutenant colonel. In 2019, Berry was inducted into the Nebraska National Guard Regional Training Institute Hall of Fame.

After transitioning from active duty, Berry applied the leadership skills he honed in the military to his legal career. A graduate of Creighton University School of Law and the prestigious Trial

Lawyers College, he has been recognized as one of the National Trial Lawyers' Top 100 trial lawyers for over a decade. Berry maintains an AV Preeminent rating from Martindale-Hubbell and has been selected as one of *U.S. News and World Report*'s Best Lawyers.

Driven by his passion for serving veterans, Berry is the CEO of Berry Law Firm, a nationwide practice dedicated to recovering back pay owed to disabled veterans. Under his guidance, the firm has secured over $350 million for more than ten thousand veterans nationwide. Berry Law's exceptional commitment to hiring and supporting veterans has earned numerous accolades, including the HIRE Vets Platinum Medallion, the Employer Support of the Guard and Reserve Pro Patria Award, recognition as a *Military Times* Best for Vets Employer, and the Better Business Bureau's Torch Award for Ethics.

Through his *Veteran Led* podcast, Berry continues his mission to inspire fellow veterans to become leaders in their communities by applying the skills forged during military service. His powerful storytelling as an author provides an authentic voice representing the struggles, triumphs, and persevering leadership embodied by America's veterans.

To learn more about veterans' disability benefits, see John's other book, *The Next Battle: A Guide to Veterans Disability Benefits*. For more on the origins of Berry Law, check out *Those Gallant Men: On Trial in Vietnam*, by John's father and the founder of Berry Law, John S. Berry Sr.

NEED FURTHER HELP?
CONNECT WITH ME ON THE FOLLOWING SITES.

YOUTUBE

Personal injury/criminal defense: @BerryLawFirm

Veteran Led: @PTSDLawyers

FACEBOOK

Veterans disability practice: @ptsdlawyers

Personal injury/criminal defense: @BerryLaw1965

Veteran Led: @veteranled

INSTAGRAM

Veterans disability practice: @ptsdlawyers

Personal injury/criminal defense: @berrylaw1965

Veteran Led: @veteranled

X

Veterans disability practice: @PTSDLawyers

Personal injury/criminal defense: @berrylaw1965

Veteran Led: @veteranled

LINKEDIN

Veterans disability practice: @berrylaw-1965

Veteran Led: @veteranled

TIKTOK

Veterans disability practice: @ptsdlawyers

Veteran Led: @veteran_led